WOMEN'S TIME USE
N RURAL TAJIKISTAN

JNE 2020

AN DEVELOPMENT BANK

ADB

© 2020 Asian Development Bank
6 ADB Avenue, Mandaluyong City, 1550 Metro Manila, Philippines
Tel +63 2 8632 4444; Fax +63 2 8636 2444
www.adb.org

Some rights reserved. Published in 2020.

ISBN 978-92-9262-236-7 (print), 978-92-9262-237-4 (electronic), 978-92-9262-238-1 (ebook)
Publication Stock No. TCS200167-2
DOI: http://dx.doi.org/10.22617/TCS200167-2

The views expressed in this publication are those of the authors and do not necessarily reflect the views and policies of the Asian Development Bank (ADB) or its Board of Governors or the governments they represent.

ADB does not guarantee the accuracy of the data included in this publication and accepts no responsibility for any consequence of their use. The mention of specific companies or products of manufacturers does not imply that they are endorsed or recommended by ADB in preference to others of a similar nature that are not mentioned.

By making any designation of or reference to a particular territory or geographic area, or by using the term "country" in this document, ADB does not intend to make any judgments as to the legal or other status of any territory or area.

Please contact pubsmarketing@adb.org if you have questions or comments with respect to content, or if you wish to obtain copyright permission for your intended use that does not fall within these terms, or for permission to use the ADB logo.

Corrigenda to ADB publications may be found at http://www.adb.org/publications/corrigenda.

Note: In this publication, "$" refers to United States dollars and "TJS" refers to somoni.

On the cover: Probing the gender divide in unpaid work reveals the invisible hands that help sustain Tajikistan's rural economy. Analysis of time use patterns within the household helps explain how rural women and men experience poverty differently (ADB photo library, Emilia Rossi, Lisa Alano).

Contents

Tables, Figures, and Boxes

Boxes

Acknowledgments

The study was carried out through the Asian Development Bank (ADB) regional technical assistance (RETA) 9088: Strengthening Gender-Inclusive Growth in Central and West Asia. The overall research process was supervised and managed by the gender and development team of the Central and West Asia Department (CWRD), composed of Mary Alice Rosero (social development and gender specialist); Gladys Puzon Franco (social development and gender officer); Gulnora Kholova (national implementation consultant of Tajikistan Resident Mission); and Maria Lisa Alano (technical assistance gender coordinator). Fritz Tadeo Tuliao (senior project analyst) provided overall administrative support. Timur Saliev of Tajikistan Resident Mission rendered administrative support to the research team in the Tajikistan. Emilia Rossi was the lead researcher and writer; Barno Kurbanova and Nigina Rajabova provided data gathering support.

The publication would not have been made possible without the full support of the CWRD management team led by Werner Liepach, director general, with support from Nianshan Zhang, deputy director general, Jesper Klindt Petersen, advisor and head of the Portfolio, Results, Safeguards and Gender Unit, and Pradeep Srivastava, Tajikistan Resident Mission country director.

We are also grateful for the valuable inputs of peer reviewers from the Gender Equity Thematic Group Nidup Tshering, senior social development officer of the Bhutan Resident Mission and Nasheeba Selim, senior social development specialist gender of the Bangladesh Resident Mission. Farrukh Nuriddinov, senior project officer of the Tajikistan Resident Mission, also reviewed and provided comments.

The team is grateful to the Tajikistan Resident Mission staff and partners from government, civil society organizations, local government, communities, and households who shared data and information in meetings, interviews, and group discussions.

Executive Summary

Tajikistan's Human Development Index value is equal to 0.656, which puts the country in the medium human development category, while poverty measures show that over 27.5% of the population in Tajikistan lives below the poverty line, which sets it among the poorest countries in Central Asia. Of the approximately 9.3 million total population, over 73% live in rural areas, and agriculture's share of the gross domestic product is about 20%.

As regards the situation of women, Tajikistan has a solid legal and policy framework for gender equality, though many agree that its implementation remains quite weak. Like other former Soviet countries, Tajikistan fares well in terms of women's education; however, negative social norms and traditional attitudes to women's status and rights within the family and society continue to limit women's opportunities and welfare. The Government of Tajikistan has stressed that inequality in opportunities is especially high for rural women, who occupy a particularly disempowered position.

A gender perspective is necessary to uncover the heterogeneous nature of poverty and its relational dimension. Applying it at the household level reveals hierarchies and inequalities in the distribution of resources, highlighting its gender dimensions. The close links between poverty and gendered inequalities in the allocation of time have been somewhat neglected, but differences in time use patterns within and across households provide important insights on how poverty is experienced by different persons, and particularly by men and women. The analysis of time use data can provide important information to inform policies and programs to alleviate poverty and tackle gender inequality. Time use surveys provide detailed information on how individuals spend their time, on a daily or weekly basis, on activities that fall within the general production boundary (paid and unpaid labor) and on personal services that are non-delegable activities.

Studies have shown that in Tajikistan, 60% of inactive labor is due to domestic responsibilities, compared to 35% in the Kyrgyz Republic and 11% in Kazakhstan. In addition, the last Asian Development Bank (ADB) Gender Assessment for Tajikistan showed that women's unpaid work is not considered in national or local economic strategy discussions and that ADB has not yet addressed time poverty in the projects it supports in the country. Gathering information on women's and men's time use is therefore necessary not only to deepen the understanding of gender norms in Tajikistan, but also to ensure that future development interventions actually benefit women and do not burden them additionally. A time use study has therefore been conducted in order to support the Government of Tajikistan in enhancing the gender and social inclusiveness of its policies and development initiatives. The study was carried out in the Khatlon region, based on its relevance for ADB programming.

The study showed that typically rural households are quite large, with 10 persons on average, and they mostly consist of extended multigenerational families. When women get married, they usually move into their husband's household, with his parents, siblings, and possibly his siblings' families. Emigration, especially labor migration of men to the Russian Federation, is a massive phenomenon in rural Tajikistan and most households have at least one family member abroad or have had one in the recent past. Families tend to have a few different sources of livelihood, which include agriculture, pensions, and remittances, as well as other forms of employment. Agriculture, however, is the main source of livelihood for most rural households and a variety of crops is produced, particularly cotton and wheat, both for the market and their own final use. It is noteworthy that even though agriculture is an essential source of livelihood, the income that families derive from it is very low.

The analysis of women's economic empowerment, which focused on women's capacity to access assets and paid economic opportunities, as well as on their role in decision-making, showed that most rural women are in a vulnerable and disempowered position, pointing at a deep gender divide. Opportunities to participate in the paid economy are very limited for rural women and only a small percentage are primary owners of agricultural land and housing. The gender analysis of time use data revealed a clear sexual division of labor, with women specializing in unpaid care and domestic activities and men specializing in productive work. The degree of specialization encountered was quite high, since for women unpaid care and domestic work represents over 70% of total work, while for men roughly the same percentage of work time is spent in paid work.

Thus, on the one hand, men specialize in paid labor, whether formally employed or not: men take up 75% of available paid labor in terms of hours worked and women account for the remaining 25%. Three-quarters of the labor force is absorbed by the agricultural sector, with about 22% having a formal job (e.g., government) and the remaining 3% engaged in other types of jobs, including construction, sales, and handicraft. Women, on the other hand, specialize in unpaid labor, which includes work for final use and domestic and care work. Unpaid work for final use includes fetching water, usually a responsibility of women; gathering wood, carried out both by men and women; as well as farm work for own final use, which differs from that for the market. While there is a stark gender disparity in terms of the access to paid work for the market, women are well represented in unpaid farm work for the household, which is associated with survival rather than income generation. In terms of direct and indirect care, women do 10 times more work than men, almost 7 hours a day. The large workload for women is explained by the high degree of gender specialization of these activities, but also by the characteristics of the households, including size of families, type of dwelling, available assets, etc. Women, especially young ones, find themselves running large rural households that require a great deal of emotional and manual labor. As in most countries worldwide, when both paid and unpaid labor are considered, rural women work longer hours than rural men in Tajikistan. The study showed that on average, rural women work almost 10 hours a day, while rural men work 8 hours a day.

The study also revealed that age is a very important factor in shaping cultural norms in rural Tajikistan. Young rural women work more than any other age group and gender, approximately 11 hours per day and, in consequence, have very little time for leisure, about half as much as young rural men. Time that women dedicate to leisure, however, increases steadily with age, and women aged 60 and older have the most leisure time, even compared to older men.

As regards decision-making on the allocation of household income, adult married men are the main decision makers in roughly one out of three cases, while women make these decisions on their own only when there are no adult men in the family (e.g., a family consisting of a widow and her children). Women, however, have higher chances of being one of the main decision makers as they get older. This is associated with existing cultural norms that assign elderly women an increasingly powerful role both in the household and the wider social sphere. These women still have many household responsibilities, but they tend to shift toward household management tasks, care of grandchildren, and other types of emotional care: they are often perceived as the "guarantors of peace and good family relations."

Political participation with respect to community organizations is low, particularly for women; however, older women also have higher chances of participating in community organizations and local government structures, provided that they are relatively well-off and educated. Three out of four women declared they voted in the last elections, while nearly all men did.

The interaction of these gender disparities in time use with employment segregation traps women in unpaid and low-paying work; an egalitarian distribution of unpaid care work among men and women is therefore key to gender equality. Interventions that lift these time constraints and increase access to the job market require action in three different areas: investment in social care and social assistance, changing social norms, and application of the legal framework for gender equality.

One of the most effective strategies to reduce and redistribute unpaid and domestic work is public investment that addresses welfare needs, including in universally accessible, high-quality care services, and social assistance like cash transfers to women, which have the potential to increase access to finance and allow women to manage finances. Social care, particularly childcare, provide a way to relax constraints on women's time. A detailed analysis of Tajikistan's care economy for various groups should therefore be undertaken. Experimentation on delivery models that address the needs of rural women should also take place, as most social care models have typically been tested in urban settings.

Another factor that greatly affects gender roles and limits women's agency is social norms. Traditional and patriarchal social norms strongly limit the decision-making power and autonomy of women in rural Tajikistan, especially in the earlier phases of their adult lives. Shifting the social norms is therefore critical and, even though this process can be complex and slow, policies can provide incentives or necessary information. To increase women's knowledge about alternatives to their daily reality, information on women's rights and existing opportunities and exposure to different female role models and the media are essential. Participation in training or vocational courses, as well as in informal groups, can also contribute to changing norms that restrict women's autonomy. A broadening of women's networks should therefore be promoted, as well as women's participation in decision-making processes.

The policy and legal framework for gender equality in Tajikistan includes the 2011–2020 National Strategy to Promote the Role of Women in the Republic of Tajikistan, the 2005 Law on State Guarantees for Gender Equality, and the 2013 Law on Domestic Violence, among other legislation. This framework is considered solid, but it lacks clear implementation processes. To improve women's agency and modify prevailing gender roles, existing equality legislation should be applied and enforced. Specific measures to facilitate access to justice for women, particularly in rural settings, should also be developed and implemented.

Finally, even when women have time available, their decision and capacity to allocate it to market work is subject to the existence of a well-functioning job market and availability of dedicated jobs. Even though identifying measures to improve the rural job market in Tajikistan is beyond the scope of this study, it should be stressed that employment for rural women is imperative for a country like Tajikistan, since market forces can sometimes also weaken social norms by compensating for the sanctions imposed for departing from them.

I. Background and Context

A. Rationale and Objectives of the Study

The present study analyzes gender inequalities in rural Tajikistan, shedding light on the unequal distribution of domestic and care work among women and men, as well as on the access to paid labor and income-generating activities. It therefore intends to examine the unequal gender relations in two rural districts in Tajikistan, both in the household and in the wider social sphere. To understand how poverty, as a multidimensional phenomenon, affects men and women differently, it is necessary to analyze the economic, social, and political autonomy of women and men.

Time use surveys (TUSs) are a unique instrument to study gender relations, as they enable measuring gender inequalities directly by looking at the different time patterns of men and women. Time is a dimension of poverty and a highly comparable one, so collecting and analyzing time use data can uncover the relationship between different socioeconomic characteristics (e.g., gender, age) and poverty. As is well known, women suffer from an excess of unpaid domestic and care work responsibilities that affect their ability to access paid labor.

Studies have shown that 60% of inactive labor in Tajikistan is due to domestic responsibilities, compared to 35% in the Kyrgyz Republic and 11% in Kazakhstan.[1] In addition, a recent analysis also revealed that rural Tajik women dedicate much more time than men to domestic and care work.[2]

The Asian Development Bank (ADB) Gender Assessment for Tajikistan showed that women's unpaid work is not considered in national or local economic strategy discussions.[3] The assessment also underlined that ADB has not yet addressed time poverty as well as health care, and gender-based violence in the projects it supports in Tajikistan. Gathering information on women's and men's time use is therefore necessary not only to deepen the understanding of gender norms, but also to ensure that development interventions actually benefit women and do not burden them additionally. Having comprehensive and comparable data is essential for the formulation of gender-responsive policies and government program interventions.

A time use study has therefore been conducted under the Technical Assistance on Strengthening Gender-Inclusive Growth in Central and West Asia (TA 9088) in order to support the Government of Tajikistan in enhancing the gender and social inclusiveness of its policies and development initiatives. The study is in line with the thrust of reducing time poverty, which is one of the five gender equality areas under ADB's Strategy 2030. The results of the study provide a basis for the inclusion of gender design features in ADB-supported projects that will reduce women's burden for domestic and care

---

[1] I. Maltseva. 2007. *Gender Equality in the Sphere of Employment*. Dushanbe: United Nations Development Fund for Women.

[2] Oxfam GB. 2018. *Using Rapid Care Analysis to Account for Time Poverty in the Zarafshan Valley, Tajikistan*. Dushanbe.

[3] Asian Development Bank (ADB). 2016. *Tajikistan Country Gender Assessment*. Manila.

work and address persistent gender roles that exacerbate gender inequalities. These may also be used to advocate for policies, programs, and social services such as institutional care services and social protection measures to promote the welfare of women engaged in unpaid care work and other unpaid economic activities that add to the family's income and resources.

B.   Context

Tajikistan's Human Development Index value is equal to 0.656, which puts the country in the medium human development category, positioning it at 125th out of 189 countries and territories.[4] Poverty measures show that over 27.5% of the population in Tajikistan live below the poverty line, which sets it among the poorest countries in Central Asia.[5]

In terms of population, approximately 9.3 million people—over 73% of the total—live in rural areas and the urbanization process is not intense as in other countries in the region.[6] Agriculture's share of the gross domestic product, about 20%, has been quite stable in the last decade, indicating a lack of structural transformation in the economy; the same holds for employment in agriculture which, according to official statistics, accounts for over 60% of the total. Agricultural jobs have the lowest productivity.[7]

When it comes to the situation of women, Tajikistan has a solid legal and policy framework for gender equality, though many agree that its implementation remains quite weak.[8] Like other former Soviet countries, Tajikistan fares well in terms of women's education, which is among the highest in Europe and Central Asia. However, negative social norms and traditional attitudes to women's status and rights within the family and society continue to limit women's opportunities and welfare.

The value of Tajikistan's 2018 Gender Inequality Index (GII) was equal to 0.377, which ranked it 84th out of 160 countries.[9] This index reflects gender-based inequalities in political representation, reproductive health, literacy, and labor market participation. According to the most recent update, in Tajikistan, 20% of parliamentary seats are held by women, and 98.8% of adult women have reached at least a secondary level of education compared to 87.0% of adult men. For every 100,000 live births, 32 women die from pregnancy-related causes, and the adolescent birth rate is 57.1 births per 1,000 women aged 15–19. Women participation in the labor market is 27.8% compared to 59.7% for men.[10] The Kyrgyz Republic and Uzbekistan ranked 87th and 64th on the GII, respectively, with their relative ranking being mostly a consequence of their national differences in terms of women's access to reproductive health and rights.

[4]   United Nations Development Programme (UNDP). 2019. *Human Development Report 2019*. New York. http://hdr.undp. org/sites/all/themes/hdr_theme/countrynotes/TJK.pdf.

[5]   Agency on Statistics under President of the Republic of Tajikistan. 2019. *Food Security and Poverty*. No. 4-2019, pp. 44 and 99.

[6]   Agency on Statistics under President of the Republic of Tajikistan. 2019. *Annual Demographic Book*. Dushanbe.

[7]   World Bank. 2017. Tajikistan Jobs Diagnostic. *Jobs Series*, 1. Washington, DC. https://openknowledge.worldbank. org/handle/10986/26029 (accessed March 2020).

[8]   Organisation for Economic Co-operation and Development (OECD). Social Institutions and Gender Index 2019, Tajikistan. https://www.genderindex.org/wp-content/uploads/files/datasheets/2019/TJ.pdf (accessed December 2019).

[9]   Footnote 4.

[10] Footnote 4.

The GII, however, does not consider dimensions like the tendency for women to work in informal and unpaid labor, including care work and agricultural work, which are women's main occupations in Tajikistan. In effect, it is widely recognized that rural women in Tajikistan occupy a particularly disempowered position: the government has stressed that inequality in opportunities is especially high for rural women, not only because of higher gender stereotypes and limited choices in the area of employment, but also due to a relatively low quality of infrastructure, which affects access to resources and opportunities.[11] The gender profile of agricultural and rural livelihoods in Tajikistan produced by the Food and Agriculture Organization of the United Nations (FAO) has stressed that women in rural areas have the least amount of free time when compared to other social groups.[12] An Oxfam study on care work in the Sughd province highlighted the constraints that women face, showing that they spend considerably more time than men in unpaid domestic and care work, and have very little time left to invest on improving their skills and knowledge and trying to access a particularly static labor market.[13]

[11] Government of Tajikistan. 2015. *National Development Strategy*. Dushanbe.
[12] Food and Agriculture Organization of the United Nations (FAO). 2016. *Gender Profile of Agricultural and Rural Livelihoods in Tajikistan*. Dushanbe.
[13] Footnote 2.

II. Understanding Gender Inequalities through Time Use Studies

A. Gender, Poverty, and Time Use

Adopting a gender perspective is essential when studying and conceptualizing poverty and elaborating effective policies and programs. The assignment of the domestic sphere to women and the public sphere to men is associated with an inequality of opportunities that prevents women from gaining access to material and social resources—including ownership of productive capital, paid labor, education, and training—and participating in decision-making in the main political, economic, and social policies. A gender perspective makes it possible to uncover the heterogeneous nature of poverty by looking into its relational dimension, both in the social sphere and in the family. As has been shown, applying a gender perspective at the household level reveals hierarchies and inequalities in the distribution of resources. Households are not homogeneous units, and different persons have different responsibilities and experiences based on their gender, age, and kin relations, among other factors.

Much has been written about the intrinsic gender dimensions of inequality, which may take different forms, ranging from income inequality; restricted social, economic, and political rights; to unequal access to and control over property and resources. However, the close links between poverty and gendered inequalities in the allocation of time have been somewhat neglected.[14]

Time is one of the most important and limited resources that people have and given that human lifetime is limited, time in any given society is a central ethical problem. Thus, the way people experience time informs analysis of economic issues, including poverty. Differences in time use patterns within and across households provide important insights on how poverty is experienced by different persons and particularly by men and women. Using a time lens makes it possible to enrich the understanding of poverty and inform alleviation strategies.[15]

The relationship between time use and poverty is also conceptualized with the term "time poverty." In broad terms, time poverty can be understood as competing claims on a person's time that constrains their ability to choose how individual time resources are allocated. This, in many cases, leads to an increased workload and to trade-offs among various tasks.[16] These may be the short-term trade-offs between different productive activities, market, and household tasks, or even restrictions on the choice of time allocation; time demand of paid or unpaid work may create severe limitations to time available for personal improvement or general well-being.

---

[14] L. Ringhofer. 2015. Time, Labour, and the Household: Measuring "Time Poverty" through a Gender Lens. *Development in Practice*. 25 (3). pp. 321–332.

[15] Öneş, U., E. Memis, and B. Kızılırmak. 2013. Poverty and Intra-Household Distribution of Work Time in Turkey: Analysis and Some Policy Implications. *Women's Studies International Forum*. 41. pp. 55–64.

[16] A. Kes and H. Swaminathan. 2006. Gender and Time Poverty in Sub-Saharan Africa. In M. Blackden and Q. Wodon, eds., *Gender, Time Use and Poverty in Sub-Saharan Africa*. Washington, DC: World Bank, pp. 13–38.

As has been widely shown, men's work is usually associated with the paid market while women devote most of their work time to unpaid work. This is particularly true in developing contexts where segregation of paid and unpaid work by gender pushes women into income poverty as well as time poverty.

The analysis of time use data can provide insights into the gendered division of labor, highlighting the unequal distribution of different paid and unpaid work. In developing countries, this information is especially important to inform poverty and gender inequality policy making. Time use studies also reveal the existence of a whole realm of human activity, namely the household system, a largely invisible domain that is unaccounted for in economic data and in the System of National Accounts. The household system can be seen as the organizational frame for human reproduction and it is typically structured as an exchange of unpaid labor, including care of children, cooking, and repair and maintenance work done on the dwelling, among other tasks. It should be noted that in rural settings, like the ones that will be analyzed in the present study, or in small-scale non-industrialized societies, economic activities may simply be an additional function of household systems.[17]

It is widely recognized that women's labor in developing countries is underrepresented in labor force statistics. Despite their significant role in domestic tasks and their contribution to the survival of rural households, survey and census data tend to underestimate women's participation in the labor market.[18] One of the causes for this misrepresentation is the definition of economic activity that often includes only income-generating activities and the production of goods and services for the market. However, the labor market is not well developed in most low- and middle-income countries and many women are excluded from it. Even though women perform work that involves time-consuming, home-based survival-related activities, this is usually overlooked in economic analysis. Many feminist economists have stressed the need to recognize the value of women's work and to develop estimates of the market value of unpaid domestic and care work. They also have argued that national accounts make a distinction between economic and non-economic activities that seem to be a product of gender biases.

For example, when the System of National Accounts (SNA) was revised in 1993, two categories of unpaid work were included within the concept of national income, but the relaxation of production boundaries was not applied to services for self-consumption. This meant the exclusion of the following items from national accounts and from calculations of gross domestic product: (i) preparation of meals, laundry, cleaning, and shopping; (ii) care of children, the elderly, the sick and people with disabilities within the household; and (iii) volunteer services provided through organizations and groups. It was recommended that the unpaid work that is excluded from the SNA production boundary be measured as extended economic work and valued in satellite accounts.[19]

The need to include care work within mainstream economics has been widely recognized. Even though the monetary valuation of these services can be problematic, attempts need to be made to find ways to incorporate them in macro policies in a meaningful way, rather than excluding them from the production boundaries.[20]

---

[17] Footnote 14.

[18] H. Zaman. 1995. Patterns of Activity and Use of Time in Rural Bangladesh: Class, Gender, and Seasonal Variations. *The Journal of Developing Areas*. 29 (3). pp. 371–388.

[19] I. Hirway. 2005. Integrating Unpaid Work into Development Policy. Paper presented at the Conference Unpaid Work and the Economy. New York: United Nations and Levy Economics Institute of Bard College.

[20] Footnote 19.

Time use surveys provide an alternative to measuring unpaid care work, as well as other economic activities, minimizing gender biases and conceptual ambiguities by simply recording time dedicated to different tasks by different household members. Box 1 contains definitions that were used as a conceptual framework for this study.

Box 1: Unpaid Work, Care Work, and Unpaid Care and Domestic Work

In order to frame the discussion, it is important to state the divide between unpaid work, care work, and unpaid care work. Definitions given by Razavi (2007) in her seminal work on care will be referred to and elaborated on.

Unpaid work includes a diverse range of activities that take place outside the cash nexus. It includes care of one's children or family, but it can also refer to unpaid work on the household plot, in the family business, or in activities such as the collection of water and firewood for self-consumption. It is interesting that while some elements of unpaid work are included in the boundaries of the System of National Accounts (SNA), for example, unpaid work in a family business, other unpaid services such as meal preparation, washing clothes, and unpaid care provided for one's child or elderly parent are excluded from the SNA and gross domestic product calculations.

Care work involves direct care of persons; it can be paid or unpaid. Direct care of persons includes bathing them, feeding them, accompanying them to the doctor, taking them for walks, talking to them, etc. Those with intense care needs include young children, the frail elderly, and people with various illnesses and disabilities. However, able-bodied adults also require and receive care, for example, supporting emotionally a friend who's mourning or simply listening to one's partner's problems at work. The activities that provide the preconditions for personal caregiving such as preparing meals, shopping, and cleaning sheets and clothes can be considered indirect care. Such boundaries are somewhat arbitrary, especially since the persons needing intensive care are often also unable to do such tasks themselves, and this is particularly true in institutional settings like orphanages or homes for the elderly. At the household level, tasks like cooking or cleaning will be considered domestic work and thus will be distinct from direct care work, strictly speaking. At the household level, these services will be referred to as domestic work. It should be noted that paid caregivers include nannies, nurses, or workers of institutions like the ones mentioned above.

Unpaid care and domestic work refers to care of persons and housework for no explicit monetary reward. If this work is not hired out to nannies or other workers, it is by definition unpaid, and it is often performed by women. Most unpaid care work in nearly all societies takes place within families, but individuals also perform unpaid care across households and across families, for other kin, friends, neighbors, and community members. In addition, unpaid care work can be carried out within a variety of institutions (public, market, not-for-profit, community) on an unpaid or voluntary basis (for example, volunteering at an orphanage or at soup kitchen).

Source: S. Razavi. 2007. The Political and Social Economy of Care in a Development Context. *Gender and Development*. Programme Paper. 3. Geneva: United Nations Research Institute for Social Development.

B.   Time Use Surveys

Time use surveys (TUSs) provide detailed information on how individuals spend their time, on a daily or weekly basis, on activities that fall within the general production boundary (paid and unpaid labor) and on personal services that are non-delegable activities. According to the United Nations Statistical Commission, time use statistics provide data that are not otherwise obtainable on human activities in the various fields of social, demographic, and related economic statistics.[21] They open up ample possibilities to understand the total economy made up of paid and unpaid work, as well as the time spent by men and women on personal activities such as human capital formation, networking and social capital formation, leisure or time stress, etc.[22]

The first time use statistics were produced in the early decades of the 1900s in social surveys of the living conditions of working-class families. The idea was to highlight time poverty of industrial workers who had long working hours and little leisure time. The usefulness of time use data in estimating and valuing unpaid work of women and women's contribution to the national economy became evident in the 1970s, when interest in gender equality and women's rights developed globally and the World Conferences on Women started taking place.[23]

In 1995, the Beijing Platform for Action appealed to countries to make visible the full extent of women's contributions to economic development by conducting regular time use studies; since then, time use data have been increasingly collected and analyzed, including in the Global South (Africa, Latin America, developing Asia, including the Middle East). Many gender experts involved in this task faced the usual challenges in mainstreaming gender-aware data collection, with political resistance and lack of gender expertise being among the most relevant.[24]

It is important to underline that the objectives of TUSs in developed and developing countries may vary somewhat. In developed countries, TUSs are useful for estimating non-SNA work, valuing unpaid work in satellite accounts, and understanding socioeconomic issues like gender inequalities. In developing countries, however, an additional TUS objective may be collecting data on SNA work, particularly informal work including home-based and subsistence work. Data collected through TUSs are also the basis for Sustainable Development Goal indicator 5.4.1 on unpaid care and domestic work. The following sections provide a brief description of the main TUS characteristics.

Type of Survey

According to United Nations guidance, time use data can be collected in three different ways: (i) independent or stand-alone surveys having the measurement of time as their specific objective; (ii) a module on time use integrated into an existing survey, such as a labor force survey or a household budget survey; and (iii) time use questions integrated with other person-level questions as part of the main questionnaire.[25]

---

[21] United Nations Statistics Division (UNSD). 2005. *Guide to Producing Statistics on Time Use: Measuring Paid and Unpaid Work.* New York.

[22] I. Hirway. 2010. *Time-Use Surveys in Developing Countries: An Assessment.* https://www.researchgate.net/publication/304636246_Time-Use_Surveys_in_Developing_Countries_An_Assessment. Accessed December 2019.

[23] Footnote 22.

[24] V. Esquivel et al. 2008. Explorations: Time Use Surveys in the South. *Feminist Economics.* 14 (3). pp. 107–52.

[25] International Labour Organization (ILO). 2018. Survey Methods to Improve Measurement of Paid and Unpaid Work: Country Practices in Time-Use Measurement. Presented at the 20th International Conference of Labour Statisticians. Geneva.

Measurement Approaches

There are three main measurement approaches available for collecting time use data: full-time diary, light-time diary, and stylized questions.[26] These traditional measurement approaches differ in costs, accuracy, as well as in their designs and applications.[27]

The main characteristic of the full-time diary method is to ask respondents to describe in their own words the activities that they engage in over a given time period. These activities are assigned codes by researchers later. The full-time diary method is usually considered to be the best practice for detailed time use data collection, as it is very accurate, but it also has high operational costs. An alternative is to use a light-time diary, which is the option that was chosen for the present study. This method can reduce costs without a big loss in terms of accuracy. Light-time diaries record the time spent in a specific pre-coded list of activities embedded into the survey instrument.

Stylized questions are used in surveys with the specific objective of capturing participation in designated activities. A typical example would be: How many hours per day (or per week) do you spend usually on activity *x*? In contrast to diary-based methods, stylized questions do not provide a complete account of time spent in all activities, but they are less expensive and can measure the incidence of specific activities, especially those occurring less frequently.

Context Variables and Simultaneous Activities

It should be noted that TUSs usually also collect information on contextual variables, that is, on the physical, social, and psychological features of the environment in which a specific activity takes place.[28] Frequently this boils down to the location where an action takes place, who was present, and for whom the activity was carried out.

In addition, TUSs may collect data on respondents' primary activity only, or also ask about simultaneous activities that are likely to generate time stress when both the performed activities simultaneously involve work. For example, if a woman cooks and simultaneously takes care of her newborn, it will be very tiring. On the other hand, if someone watches TV and has lunch along with it, this will probably be relaxing. It is therefore necessary to analyze and address simultaneous activities by their nature. These data are particularly useful to understand the time stress of women, particularly of poor women.[29]

---

[26] Direct observation is an additional possible measurement approach, but it is usually more used by individual researchers and with small and geographically limited samples.

[27] UNSD. 2018. Modernizing Time Use Surveys. Paper Presented at the International Forum on Gender Statistics. Tokyo.

[28] UNSD. 2005. *Guide to Producing Statistics on Time Use: Measuring Paid and Unpaid Work*. New York.

[29] I. Hirway. 2010. *Time-Use Surveys in Developing Countries: An Assessment*. https://www.researchgate.net/publication/304636246_Time-Use_Surveys_in_Developing_Countries_An_Assessment (accessed December 2019).

Classification of Activities

The classification of activities is particularly relevant for diary methods in terms of the international comparability of data, and it forms an integral component of any TUS. Currently, there is no single international standard classification of activities and numerous frameworks being used, which naturally limits the international comparability of the data. Examples of the varying frameworks include

- American Time Use Study classification,

- Australian Time Use Activity Classification,

- Harmonised European Time Use Survey, and

- International Classification of Activities for Time Use Statistics (ICATUS).

The ICATUS can be considered an umbrella classification that was developed with the intention of keeping in mind the needs of developing countries. It is adaptable to countries' own context by expanding categories and was conceived on the initiative of the UN Statistical Commission, following the recommendation of the Beijing Platform for Action. It was established with the support of an international expert group through a long trial process that ended in 2016. As explained below, this classification was referred to and adapted for the present study.

Coverage

A review by the International Labour Organization (ILO) identified 117 unique sources of time use data collected in 94 countries from 2000 to 2016.[30]

In the developed world, Europe has the longest tradition in terms of TUSs, which are mostly stand-alone surveys (not modules) carried out periodically. The United States (US) and Canada also have periodical independent TUSs, as well other developed countries like Japan, New Zealand, and Australia.[31]

In the Global South, the situation is quite different. Of the 54 countries of the African Union, around 30 countries, or 57%, have carried out at least one TUS; of the 44 member countries of the United Nations Economic Commission for Latin America and the Caribbean, 18–20 countries, or 42%–45%, have conducted at least one survey. In the Asia and the Pacific region, 24 developing and emerging countries have conducted at least one TUS.[32] At the moment, a TUS has never been carried out in Tajikistan and only a local rapid care assessment exists.[33] This pilot survey therefore constitutes the first attempt to collect time use statistics in the country.

---

[30] ILO. 2018. Survey Methods to Improve Measurement of Paid and Unpaid Work: Country Practices in Time-Use Measurement. Presented at the 20th International Conference of Labour Statisticians. Geneva.

[31] J. Charmes. 2015. *Time Use Across the World: Findings of a World Compilation of Time Use Surveys*. Background Paper. UNDP Human Development Report Office.

[32] ILO and UNDP. 2018. *Time-use Surveys and Statistics in Asia and the Pacific*. Geneva: ILO.

[33] Footnote 2.

III. Methodological Approach

The methodological approach for this study relied mainly on quantitative research methods and specifically on the collection and analysis of time use and other socioeconomic data via a time use study (TUS). Additionally, qualitative in-depth interviews were carried out to complement and deepen the survey's results. This section describes the approach adopted in this study focusing on the TUS, which represented the bulk of the research.

A.   Scope and Objectives of the Survey

The objective of the TUS in rural Tajikistan was to collect data on the time that men and women in rural households spend engaged in different activities. It specifically aimed at data that would enable performing a gender analysis of time use patterns, with a focus on paid and unpaid work. Methodologically, the rural Tajikistan TUS was a stand-alone pilot survey, implemented through face-to-face interviews and carried out by trained enumerators.

Administratively, Tajikistan is divided into five regions: Dushanbe, Districts of Republican Subordination, Sughd, Khatlon, and Gorno–Badakhshan. Each region is subdivided into districts. The Khatlon region was prioritized for this study because it is the largest horticulture producer in the country. Within this region, the targeted districts for the survey were Khuroson and Jaihun.

For the sake of this study, areas with no relevant population agglomerations where the main livelihood is derived from agriculture are defined as rural. There is no internationally agreed upon definition of rural, but many definitions set the threshold for population agglomerations at 10,000.[34] There are some small towns in the selected districts with population of over 10,000, including Khuroson and Jaihun. Households within the borders of these towns were not included in the sample.

As regards the concept of household, it is based on the arrangements made by persons, individually or in groups, for providing themselves with food or other essentials for living.[35] This includes sharing common household expenses or daily needs and a shared residence. A household can include either one person living alone or a group of people, not necessarily related, living at the same address with common housekeeping, i.e., sharing at least one meal per day or sharing a living or sitting room.

This definition of household was used in the present study; however, some flexibility was applied to the residence criterion for migrant family members. Family members who were abroad at the time of

---

[34] Rural areas can also be defined as non-urban, with urban areas in Tajikistan being defined as "cities and urban-type localities, officially designated as such, usually according to the criteria of number of inhabitants and predominance of agricultural, or number of non-agricultural workers and their families." https://unstats.un.org/unsd/demographic/sconcerns/densurb/Defintion_of Urban.pdf (accessed December 2019).

[35] OECD. Glossary of Statistical Terms. https://unstats.un.org/unsd/demographic/sconcerns/densurb/Defintion_of Urban.pdf (accessed December 2019).

survey were not interviewed; however, persons who were temporarily working abroad and contributing to household income were considered household members, even if they had been abroad for over 3 months, the reference threshold. The relaxation of the concept of household membership stemmed from the need to adapt to the local context encountered during the pre-test phase. Families tend to consider migrant relatives from whom they receive remittances and that are away temporarily as household members. In Tajikistan, the most common profile of an international migrant is that of a young or middle-aged man temporarily migrating to the Russian Federation, leaving his wife and children behind living with his parents. In this typical case, the migrant was considered a household member. Persons living in institutions (prisons, hospitals, military bases, etc.) were not included in the present study.

B. Sampling Design

The total sample size was initially defined based on cost considerations, estimating that a maximum of 72 households could be surveyed in the available time and resources. The sample size of a TUS can be expanded with the least cost by selecting all members of a sample household (older than a certain age); even though there is a high variability across countries, many TUSs take this approach. In the present survey, all men and women aged 20 or older who are permanent residents of the sampled households were considered eligible to be interviewed, and three persons per household were selected. The total sample size was therefore determined to be equal to 216, that is, three persons in each of the 72 selected households.

As mentioned, the Khatlon region was selected because of its relevance in terms of agricultural production. Within this region, the two districts of Khuroson and Jaihun were targeted based on their importance to ADB's programming, specifically an upcoming irrigation program. Given the available time and resources, the sampling design aims at collecting data that are representative of these districts; however, considering the relative homogeneity of Khatlon's rural areas, generalizations can be extended to the regional level.

Most samples for national household TUSs are drawn systematically using multi-stage stratified random sampling techniques.[36] This requires information from the census on enumeration areas in each selected geographical unit and lists of households belonging to each unit to be systematically selected. The Agency on Statistics under President of the Republic of Tajikistan divides each district into census divisions, which are subdivided into instruction areas. Each instruction area is divided into urban enumeration areas or rural villages, also called primary sampling units (PSUs). The sampling frame of the most recent surveys (e.g., 2017 Tajikistan Demographic and Health Survey) is based on this list of PSUs.

Given the resources and time constraints, it was not possible to carry out a random selection from the PSU lists of each district; therefore, it was not possible to create a probability sample and the marginal sampling error could not be calculated. However, several steps were taken to avoid high levels of bias.

To guarantee that the sample is representative of certain social groups that are relevant to the TUS objectives, a quota sampling approach was used. This means that the representation of said groups in the sample is proportional to their representation in the actual population, based on data available from the statistics office. The variables that were considered most relevant in the survey are gender

[36] ILO and UNDP. 2018. *Time-use Surveys and Statistics in Asia and the Pacific*. Geneva: ILO.

and age; hence, they were used to establish the quotas. It was assumed that the distribution of the national Tajik population by sex and age group, shown in Table 1, was also valid at the district level.[37]

Table 1: Tajik Population: Percentage Distribution by Sex and Age Group, 2018

Age Group	Male	Female	Total
20–29	16.7	16.3	33.0
30–44	17.6	17.5	35.1
45–59	10.6	11.0	21.6
Over 60	4.9	5.4	10.3
Total	**49.8**	**50.2**	**100.0**

Source: Agency on Statistics under President of the Republic of Tajikistan—TajStat.

The sampling quotas were defined as shown in Table 2. The sample was split evenly between the two districts given the relevance of both districts for ADB activities.

Table 2: Sampling Quotas by Age Group and Sex

Age Group	Male	Female	Total
20–29	36	38	74
30–44	35	35	70
45–59	25	27	52
Over 60	10	10	20
Total	**106**	**110**	**216**

Source: Author's computation.

In order to have a sample that represented areas where the presence or absence of irrigation systems was a relevant issue, a component of intentional sampling was added to the approach. Therefore, within Khuroson and Jaihun, subdistrict (*jamoats*) were prioritized in order to include areas where irrigation is available and where it is not (or no longer).

Finally, a system of prioritization was specified to select household respondents and ensure that the data collected enable adequately representing gender relations. The concept of head of household was not used in this survey and the primary respondent in each household was specified as the household reference woman.

Since most households in Tajikistan are made up of either nuclear or extended multigenerational families, the household reference woman was identified as the married woman[38] who is in the central

---

[37] Clearly the distribution of population by sex and age group in rural areas might differ from the national level, but sex-disaggregated data at the district or even regional level were not readily available. These data are not currently published, even though they are certainly collected in the census. It should be noted that over 70% of Tajik population is rural; hence, the rural population is well represented in national figures.

[38] According to the last Demographic and Health Survey (TSI, 2017) nearly three-quarters of women (72%) are currently married or living together with a partner as though married, while 22% of women have never been married. Six percent of women are divorced, separated, or widowed. The figures refer to women aged 15 to 49.

stages of the life cycle, i.e., she usually has children and her elderly parents are alive. In households that only include a nuclear family, i.e., a couple that is married or living together with their children, the household reference woman is the wife/female partner. Households that are made of multigenerational extended families, i.e., one or more nuclear families, and other relatives are extremely common in rural Tajikistan. In this type of household, one of the married women was randomly chosen as the reference woman. The second respondent and third respondent were eligible household members that made it possible to complete the sample quotas. In most cases, this meant interviewing two women and one man, or two men and one woman in each household.

As regards the TUS period of reference, this is usually a year, so surveys tend to be conducted in different moments during the chosen year and, therefore, factor in possible seasonality. It should be noted, however, that many TUSs in developing countries, even at the national level, do not do this. In the present survey, data collection took place over October and November; the reference period is therefore the fall season. Since the surveyed areas are rural, it can be expected that some variation exists in terms of agricultural work. Winter tends to be a much slower period if compared to others; work picks up in spring and summer, which are the busiest seasons since planting and harvesting activities take place. Fall is also a time to harvest some crops, as well as a period to prepare the land and the household for winter, including to collect wood. In the in-depth interviews, some questions on how seasons affect work were asked, but time use seasonality was not quantified.

Many national TUSs sample the days to be surveyed as well, using a reference day for the time use data that will be collected. In this survey, the reference day was not sampled. The methodological approach for this survey consisted of asking respondents to refer to a typical day and an atypical one, which correspond respectively to a weekday and to a weekend day. Sunday was considered the only weekend day, as in the pre-test phase it emerged that Saturday was not considered to be in any way different from the rest of the week, as many children go to school and farm work and other work is also done. For the typical day, respondents were asked to recall what they did the day before the interview, the so-called recall method, with the enumerator recording and coding the responses. For the atypical day, respondents were asked to recall what they did last Sunday. Adjustments were made when interviews were done on Mondays.

C.   Survey Instrument and Implementation

Based on the objectives and scope of the survey, an ad hoc instrument was developed. The survey was implemented through face-to-face interviews, administered by trained Tajik enumerators with a paper and pen instrument.

Besides the time diary, the survey instrument included a background questionnaire and was divided in two parts. Part 1 consists of a household questionnaire, while part 2 is made up of an individual questionnaire and a light-time diary. The background household questionnaire includes a section on household composition, a section on the dwelling and a section on the household economy. The background individual questionnaire enquires about the main socioeconomic variables (e.g., ethnic group, migrant status, age).

The light-time diary is a 24-hour diary that contains a list of pre-coded activities developed especially for this survey. The reference activity classification used in the survey instrument is a simplified and adapted version of the ICATUS, that was perfected in the pre-test phase. The final version of the activity classification is available in Appendix 1. It is worth noting that even among experts there is no agreement on whether international harmonization (the building of a satisfactory common ground in terms of methods and activity classifications as a prerequisite for performing international comparisons) should take precedence over catering to specific local needs.[39] In the Tajik TUS, a mixed approach was taken, allowing for a certain international comparability, but also adapting to the local context and survey characteristics.

The time diary is made up of 30 minutes intervals and starts at 4 a.m. The instrument included questions on a possible simultaneous activities and contextual variables. These data are not easy to collect and analyze, as confirmed by the pre-test in Tajikistan, hence many countries do not do it. However, given the nature of the survey, a pilot and relatively small initiative, an effort was made to collect data on one secondary simultaneous activity and one contextual variable, i.e., the location of the activity being recorded.

Survey procedures developed for enumerators included indications on how to manage the data collection process, ensuring the methodological approach was respected. The enumerators received specific training and participated in the pre-test.

To elicit cooperation and interest in the survey, the research team met with the district-level government entities; local women's committees were also critically involved. During the period dedicated to actual data collection, enumerators prepared weekly schedules. Prior to the interview, enumerators contacted households to explain survey objectives and the importance of time use data. They also explained the importance of responding in relation to being selected and scheduled the visit. The personal questionnaires and diaries were personal and could be answered only by the selected respondent and not by someone else on their behalf, so proxy reporting was not allowed.

D.   Key Outputs of Time Use Survey and International Comparability of Results

As with any other survey, data collected through a TUS are organized and summarized in statistical tables, with estimates of population characteristics. A TUS focuses on people's activities during the 24-hour course a day and the duration of the activities.[40]

Typically, the indicators published by TUSs are of three types:

- the average daily time spent in a given activity of the classification by the population engaged (or involved) in the activity;

- the participation rate (the number of people engaged in the activity divided by the total population—engaged or not—of the sample); and

- the average daily time spent in a given activity by the total population, engaged or not in the activity.[41]

---

[39] V. Esquivel et al. 2008. Explorations: Time Use Surveys in the South. *Feminist Economics*. 14 (3). pp. 107–52.

[40] UNSD. 2005. *Guide to Producing Statistics on Time Use: Measuring Paid and Unpaid Work*. New York.

[41] J. Charmes. 2015. *Time Use Across the World: Findings of a World Compilation of Time Use Surveys*. Background Paper. UNDP Human Development Report Office.

In this report, most figures refer to the third of these three indicators; however, participation rates for paid and unpaid work will also be provided in Appendix 3 as a reference.

It is worth noting that comparability of international results depends on a number of factors, including age limits defined for the sample, as well as location (rural/urban): when people over aged 14 are included in samples, there tends to be more time spent learning; in urban areas commuting can take up a good chunk of people's days, which is usually not the case in rural areas. In other words, that the Tajikistan survey focused on rural areas, and that people aged 20 or older were eligible to be part of the sample, does affect its results, which are comparable with national figures only up to certain point. However, the international comparability of the survey was kept in mind when designing the methodological approach, which purposefully refers to an international classification of activities and to methodological advice provided by international statistical entities (i.e., United Nations Statistics Division, United Nations Economic Commission for Europe, ILO).

E.   Qualitative Interviews

In order to deepen the understanding of the gendered organization of household members' daily activities, the pilot TUS was complemented by qualitative research. The qualitative approach relied on semi-structured, face-to-face, in-depth interviews, mainly with women living in rural households of the targeted districts; it did, however, include some men. Two group discussions with women were also carried out.

Interview guides focused on the organization of paid and unpaid work but also of leisure time, community participation, and socializing. Intra-household power relations and the relationship between women's excess of care responsibilities and the access to paid labor were also explored.

The interviews took place in December after the completion of the TUS.

IV. An Overview of the Sample

Typically, rural households in this area of Tajikistan are quite large, with on average four children and six adults, possibly including disabled or elderly family members and migrant members who are temporarily abroad. When women get married, they usually move in with their husband's family, including his parents and possibly his siblings, so most households are made up of extended multigenerational families, while nuclear families are a minority. Labor migration is a massive phenomenon, particularly for men, and in most rural households there is at least one migrant family member abroad or there has been one in the recent past.

Most rural families live in a detached house or in several small detached houses opening on the same common yard, with an outdoor latrine, a home garden, and a stall for farm animals. Access to drinking and cooking water is somewhat problematic: rural families either buy water from trucks or they collect it from irrigation canals and public pipes. Rainwater is also used as a secondary water source. Families often rely on traditional fuels like wood or animal dung for cooking, but gas and electricity are also widely used and access to the latter is nearly universal. Clothes are washed by hand in the great majority of households, as only one out of four households has a washing machine. Nearly all households own a TV, but only one out of seven has access to the internet, mainly through a mobile connection. Households tend to have at least a few different sources of livelihood, which include agriculture, pensions, and remittances, as well as other forms of employment. Even though the income they derive from it is very low, agriculture is the main source of livelihood for most rural households and a variety of crops is produced, particularly cotton and wheat, both for the market and the family's final use.

The analysis of women's economic empowerment, which focused on women's capacity to access assets and paid economic opportunities, as well as on their role in decision-making, showed that most rural women are in a vulnerable and disempowered position, pointing at a deep gender divide. Opportunities to participate in the paid economy are very limited for rural women and only a small percentage are primary owners of agricultural land and housing. The main occupation for most women is unpaid care and domestic work, while for men it is agriculture, reflecting the typical sexual division of labor. This gender divide also emerges clearly when decisions on household income are analyzed. In the majority of households, decisions on income allocation are taken jointly, either by the main couple or by various household members, but in many families the main decision maker is an adult married man. It is noteworthy that as women get older their power in the household increases greatly, they become highly respected and perceived as being essential to ensure smooth functioning of the household and family relations.

Political participation in respect to community organizations, however, is low, even for older women, unless they are relatively well-off and educated.

A. Sociodemographic Profile of Households and Respondents

The surveyed households were in general quite large and mainly included extended families (81.9%), which tends to be the norm in rural Tajikistan, and, to a lesser extent (18.1%), nuclear families (Figure 1). Extended families are generally multigenerational and include one or more married couples as well as their children. The household will usually also include one or more elderly persons, often the parents of one of the married men.

Figure 1: Households by Family Type

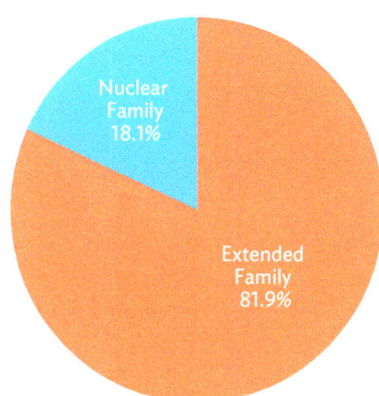

Source: Author's computation based on 2019 time use survey results.

As shown in Table 3, the surveyed households have on average 10 members, including typically 3 adult women, 2 adult men, and 4 children. Over half of the households had migrant family members abroad at the time of the survey. As specified in the methodology, migrant family members were considered part of the household when they contributed to household income, even if they were not present at the time of the interview.

As mentioned, the overwhelming majority of Tajik migrants are men, and women who emigrate usually follow their husbands (Figure 2). Married men who go to work abroad mostly leave their wives and children in Tajikistan and they continue contributing to the household budget through remittances.

Table 3: Composition of Household: Average Number of Members

Adults male	2.9
Adults female	3.1
Children	4.1
Total Household	**10.1**

Source: Author's computation based on 2019 time use survey results.

Figure 2: Share of Households with Current or Former Migrant Family Members

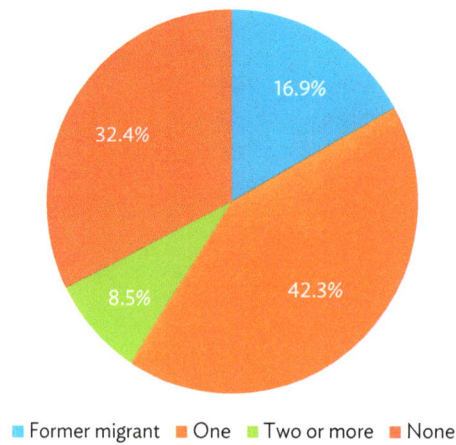

16.9%
32.4%
8.5%
42.3%

■ Former migrant   ■ One   ■ Two or more   ■ None

Source: Author's computation based on 2019 time use survey results.

Very few of the interviewed women (2%) had the experience of being migrant workers abroad, whereas about 18% of male respondents had done so in the last 3 years and had then decided to return home. When women migrate, it is usually to follow their husband; autonomous migration is not at all common for Tajik women as it is in other Asian countries.

There also is a well-known phenomenon of women who are abandoned by their migrant husbands. Even though the survey was not specific enough to enquire into this phenomenon, the qualitative interviews highlighted two cases of abandoned women, who ended up returning to their family of origin. In both cases, the rejection was associated to an actual or perceived disability of the woman: one of the women was repudiated by her husband after getting ill and suffering a lower body paralysis, while the other one was rejected because of a supposed inability to get pregnant.

Figure 3: Share of Households with a Dependent Adult or Person with Disability

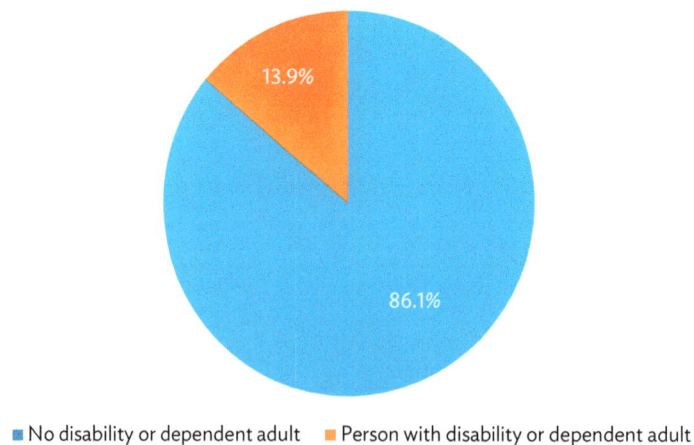

13.9%
86.1%

■ No disability or dependent adult   ■ Person with disability or dependent adult

Source: Author's computation based on 2019 time use survey results.

As regards actual disability, the survey showed that in about 14% of surveyed households there was either a person with a disability or a dependent adult, usually an older person, who requires additional care (Figure 3).

As regards the place of origin of respondents, almost three-quarters were born in the district where they live (Figure 4). The remaining persons mainly come from another district in the Khatlon region, which accounts for 90% of the sample. As shown in Figure 5, ethnically, interviewees are 86% Tajik and 14% Uzbek. In terms of their marital status, most respondents are married (87%) and there are more widowed women than men in the sample, which can be associated with Tajik men's shorter life expectancy compared to women (Figure 6). The average age of marriage for women is 19.3 years, while for men it is 23.7 years.

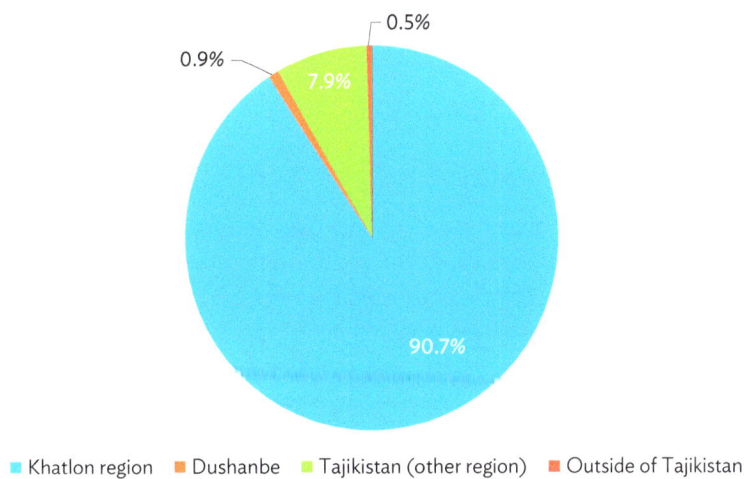

Figure 4: Share of Respondents by Place of Birth

- 0.5%
- 0.9%
- 7.9%
- 90.7%

■ Khatlon region ■ Dushanbe ■ Tajikistan (other region) ■ Outside of Tajikistan

Source: Author's computation based on 2019 time use survey results.

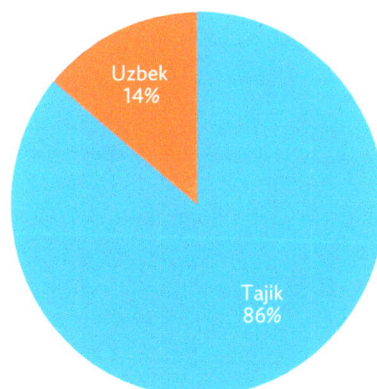

Figure 5: Ethnic Origin of Respondents

- Uzbek 14%
- Tajik 86%

Source: Author's computation based on 2019 time use survey results.

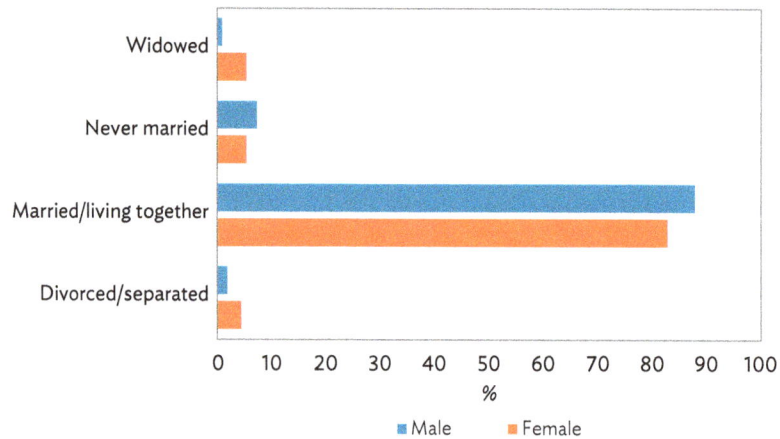

Figure 6: Share of Respondents by Marital Status

Source: Author's computation based on 2019 time use survey results.

B.   Housing Conditions, Services, and Assets

As regards the type of dwelling, about 54% of households are made up of more than one house (i.e., building) where different persons live, while 25% are semi-detached houses, and about 20.8% are single-detached houses. It should be noted that even though the idea of a semi-detached house is associated with having different households in each part of the house, in this survey, it was different nuclear families of the same extended family who were splitting a house in two. The extended family then shares food and income, thereby making up a household.

The roof and walls of the dwellings tend to be in a great majority of cases finished. However, the floors of dwellings are rudimentary or natural (earth, adobe, or wood planks) in one out of three households and finished in the other cases. In line with official statistics on toilet facilities in rural settings, none of the surveyed households have flush toilets; instead they all have pit latrines for the exclusive use of their members, as well as electricity, provided by the governmental power supplier.

As regards water, there tends to be several sources that vary with the season. When asked to identify the main source of drinking and washing water, 54.9% of households declared that they buy water from water trucks or carts, 6.3% get water from a public pipe, and 38.9% use the irrigation canal (Figure 7). A secondary source of household water that was identified through qualitative interviews is rainwater.

In two out of three households, it is women who are in charge of fetching water for the household and, to a lesser extent, young boys (17%) and adult men (13%). It should be noted that when water is bought from trucks, it is usually ordered and then delivered to the household, where it is stored in a tank; adult men are generally involved in the purchase of water and the organization of its delivery. Women or male youths are usually in charge of actually collecting the water.

The survey showed that families use different sources of fuel for cooking or a mix of these. As shown in Figure 8, more than half of the households use either electricity or wood for cooking, at least sometimes. Gas is used by 44% of households and animal dung by 9.7%. Some differences also

Figure 7: Main Source of Drinking Water, Washing Water, and Cooking Water

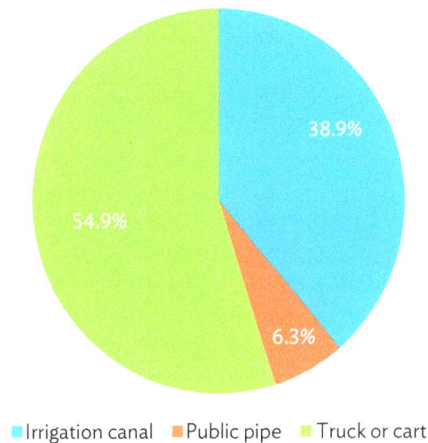

- 38.9%
- 54.9%
- 6.3%

■ Irrigation canal ■ Public pipe ■ Truck or cart

Source: Author's computation based on 2019 time use survey results.

Figure 8: Fuel for Cooking—Share of Households Using Different Sources

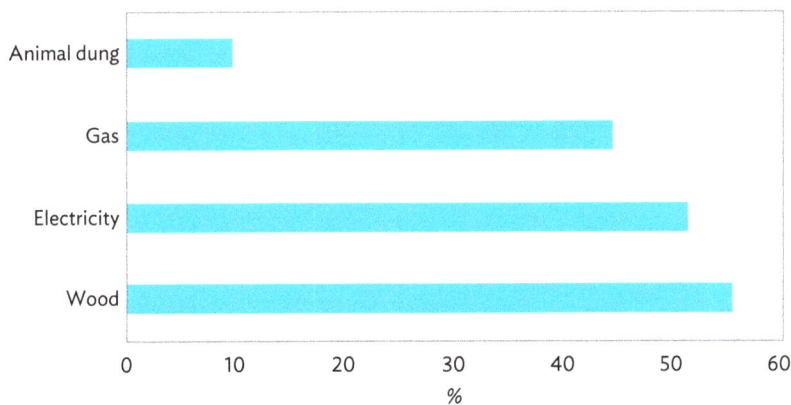

Source: Author's computation based on 2019 time use survey results.

emerged between districts: in Jaihun, most households use a mix of wood and electricity, the latter for preparing breakfast and the former for preparing lunch; in Khuroson, the main type of fuel is gas, while animal dung is also mentioned as an alternative cooking fuel by some families.

As regards ownership of the house (Figure 9), in more than two out of three households the dwelling is owned by the husband of the main married couple, whereas the household reference woman is the owner of the dwelling in only 9.7% of cases. In the remaining cases, the house is owned jointly by the main married couple (nearly 1.4%), by the parents or parents-in-law (16.7%), or by another household member (1.4%). These data are expressed in terms of the relation of the owner of the house to the reference woman; hence, the category "parents" will usually correspond to the parents-in-law since traditionally women move into their husband's household when they get married. All the surveyed households declared that they have a title for the house they live in.

Figure 9: Ownership of House in Relationship to Household Reference Woman (Wife)

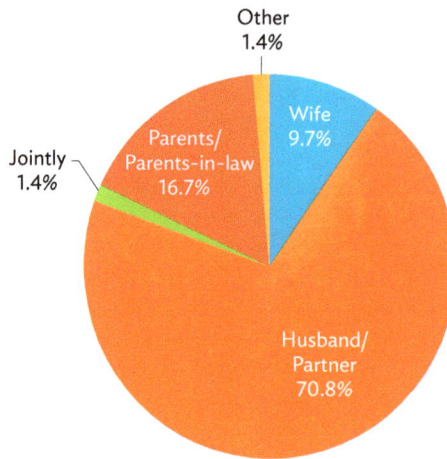

- Other 1.4%
- Wife 9.7%
- Parents/Parents-in-law 16.7%
- Jointly 1.4%
- Husband/Partner 70.8%

Source: Author's computation based on 2019 time use survey results.

As shown in Table 4, in terms of assets and services, electricity and television are available to all surveyed households. Refrigerators are owned by most households, as are irons, whereas washing machines are available only to one out of four households. Computers are owned by 8.3% of the households, whereas 15.3% of households declare that they have access to the internet at home, which is usually through their mobile phones. This figure is in line with individual responses on internet access.

Table 4: Share of Households Owning Different Assets/Having Access to Services (%)

Assets/Services	%
Electricity	100.0
Television	100.0
Iron	95.8
Refrigerator	84.7
Bicycle	75.0
Car	55.6
Other (e.g., wheelbarrow)	51.4
Washing machine	23.6
Radio	15.3
Internet	15.3
Vacuum cleaner	13.9
Computer	8.3
Motorbike	1.4

Source: Author's computation based on 2019 time use survey results.

C.   Household Economy

Rural families tend to have diverse sources of livelihood: 9 out of 10 surveyed households base their survival on at least two sources. This is not surprising given the size of families, which increases the possibility of different members having access to different occupations and sources of income. These include agriculture, pensions, and remittances, as well as other forms of employment and business.

If only the main source of livelihood is considered (Figure 10), then 64% of surveyed households rely primarily on agriculture for their survival and reproduction, 28% on remittances, and 8% on income deriving from some other kind of employment or business.

However, if all the different sources of livelihood mentioned by respondents are considered (Figure 11), almost all the households recur in some measure to agriculture, whether in the form of production

Figure 10: Main Source of Livelihood—Share of Households

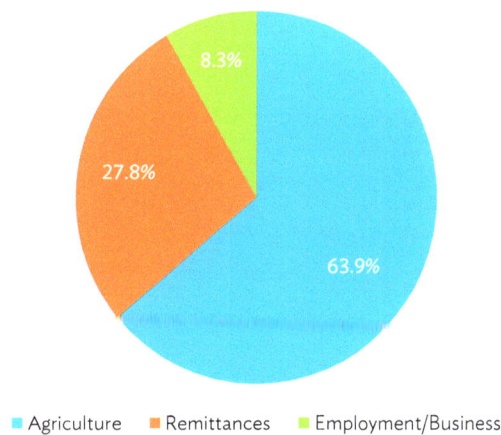

Source: Author's computation based on 2019 time use survey results.

Figure 11: Mentioned Sources of Livelihood—Share of Households

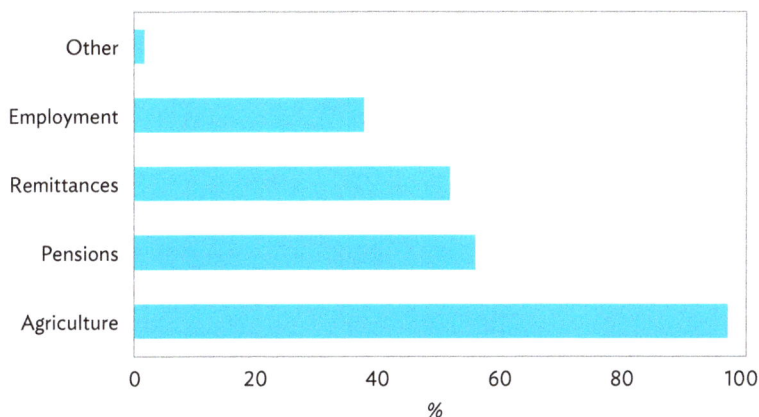

Source: Author's computation based on 2019 time use survey results.

for final use or for the market. Remittances or pensions (old age or other social pensions) are also mentioned as a source of livelihood by at least half of the surveyed households. Different types of employment and business generate incomes that support over a third of families.

The great majority of surveyed households have access to agricultural land, the median agricultural land area being equal to 3 hectares, including both home gardens and agricultural land.[42]

It should be noted that in Tajikistan access to land has a specific legal meaning, i.e., there is no private land ownership, but individuals have the right to use land through land tenure. Hence, in line with other studies on the subject, ownership of land is understood in this report as the right to use land conveyed to individuals whose names are included on land certificates and licenses.[43]

As shown in Figure 12, in more than half of the cases, the agricultural land that is available to these families is the property of one of the adult married men of the household; only in 6% of cases does the household reference woman own the land directly. It should be noted that in about one out of three households the property of the land is of another household member, including parents or parents-in-law. This is consistent with the fact that most rural households are made up of extended families that include on average five to six adults. Certificates are the main form of title for land.

The agricultural land that households have access to is in most cases (94%) only irrigated in part, which means that families might have a plot that is irrigated, including their home garden, and then other land that is not. The method of irrigation is mostly traditional, but in a handful of households, drip irrigation was also present, thanks to an international aid program. Qualitative interviews showed

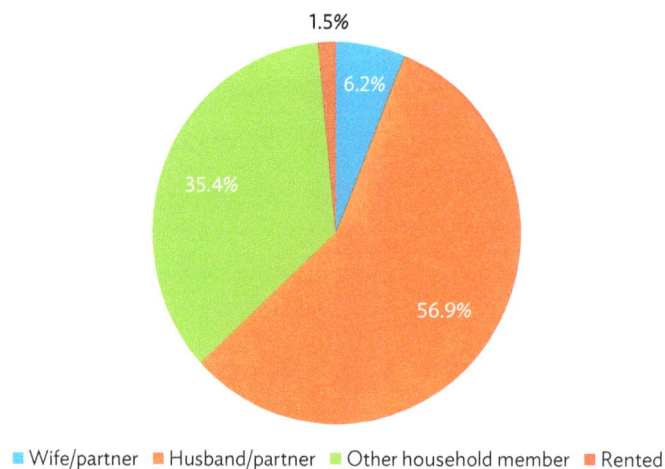

Figure 12: Ownership of Agricultural Land by Household Member

Source: Author's computation based on 2019 time use survey results.

[42] Agricultural land is defined as the land area that is either arable, under permanent crops, or under permanent pastures. Arable land includes land under temporary crops such as cereals, temporary meadows for mowing or for pasture, land under market or kitchen gardens, and land temporarily fallow. Land abandoned as a result of shifting cultivation is excluded.
[43] Footnote 12.

that some people decide to return part of their non-irrigated land to the state when they are unable to make it profitable and it becomes a source of debt.

In term of crops produced (Figure 13), two out of three households grow cotton on at least part of their land. Wheat (62.1%) is the second most frequent crop, followed by clover (36.4%). When asked whether women of the household grow specific crops in the home garden or on the farm (Figure 14), over half of the households specified at least one crop. The crops mostly mentioned are vegetables (75%), fruit trees (40%), and potatoes (22.5%).

Only 14% of surveyed households own a tractor or other mechanical equipment. In most cases, this is owned and operated by one of the adult men of the household.

Figure 13: Crops Produced—Share of Total Households

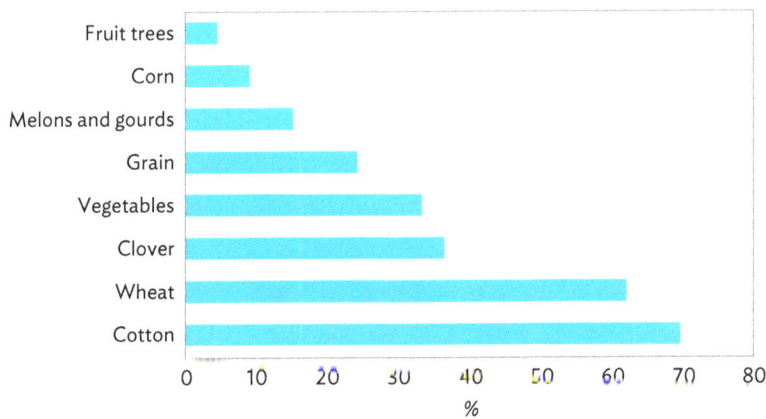

Source: Author's computation based on 2019 time use survey results.

Figure 14: Crops Produced by Women—Share of Households Where Women Produce Specific Crops

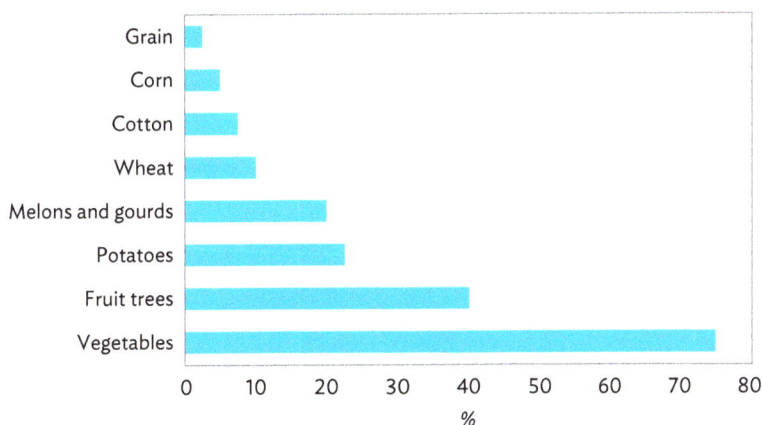

Source: Author's computation based on 2019 time use survey results.

Raising farm animals is also the norm for rural families and over 90% of households own livestock. There is no specific ownership system for livestock, which is considered a common property of the household; however, it is mostly traded by men, as market access in rural areas is usually the responsibility of men. In most households, women are also involved in the management and care of farm animals, with specific responsibilities, as will be discussed in section V.

As shown in Table 5, in terms of the estimated household income, the survey shows that households have an average monthly income equal to TJS1,787 (about $180). The average income is significantly higher in households where the main source of livelihood is formal employment (TJS2,383) than in households where the main source of livelihood is agriculture (TJS1,667). Average income is also slightly higher in households that have at least one family member currently working abroad (TJS1,864) than in households with no migrants abroad (TJS1,713).[44] Thus, even though agriculture is an important source of livelihood for most rural families, the income that is derived from it is very low.

Table 5: Average Household Monthly Income by Main Source of Livelihood (TJS)

Livelihood Source	Income
Agriculture	1,667
Employment/Business	2,383
Remittances	1,884
Total	**1,787**

Source: Author's computation based on 2019 time use survey results.

D.   Economic Empowerment and Political Participation

The role in decision-making on the allocation of income, as well as the capacity to access assets and paid economic opportunities, are fundamental indicators of women's economic empowerment.[45] The analysis of ownership presented above showed that women who are the primary owners of agricultural land and housing are a small minority. The figures below show that women's opportunities to participate in the paid economy in rural Tajikistan are also very limited, pointing at a deep gender divide. This divide also emerges clearly when decisions on spending household income are analyzed and it reflects the typical sexual division of labor that will be examined in depth in section V on time use.

As shown in Figure 15, when asked about their main occupation, 46.3% of individuals identified agriculture as their primary economic activity, confirming the household-level analysis on sources of livelihood. However, if the data are disaggregated by sex, women are mostly busy with unpaid care and domestic work (73.6%), while men are concentered in the agricultural sector (72.6%) and other productive occupations, including professional or technical jobs (13.2%), as well as manual labor (4.7%).

---

[44] It should be noted that, according to enumerators, interviewees were reticent to reveal income generated and some responses did not seem very plausible, hence this data should be read and interpreted with some caution.

[45] N. Kabeer. 2012. Women's Economic Empowerment and Inclusive Growth: Labour Markets and Enterprise Development. *Soas Discussion Paper* 29/12. https://www.soas.ac.uk/cdpr/publications/papers/file80432.pdf (accessed December 2019).

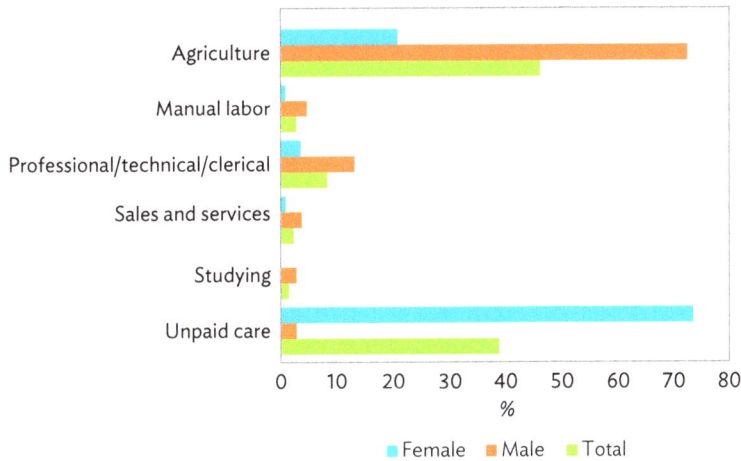

Figure 15: Main Occupation—Share of Respondents, by Sex and Total

Source: Author's computation based on 2019 time use survey results.

It should be noted that most individuals do not receive a payment from their main occupation. For women, this is clearly the case as overwhelmingly they are doing unpaid care and domestic work, guaranteeing the survival and reproduction of their families. Men, on the other hand, usually do not receive a payment for their work on the family farm as profits may be managed by the head of the household. As a result, they may go back into the family business or the work carried out could be aimed simply at producing crops and raising livestock for the household's final use.

In addition, if only occupations that can generate an income are considered (Figure 16), i.e., if studying and unpaid care are excluded, about 73% of respondents declared that they do not receive a payment for their main occupation, as it is carried out for the family business of for final use.

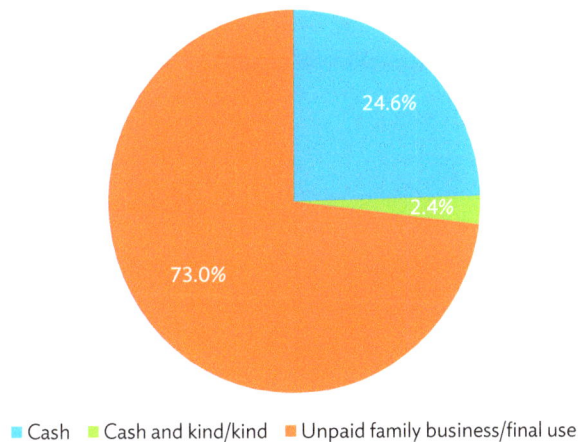

Figure 16: Type of Payment for Productive Occupations—Share of Respondents

Source: Author's computation based on 2019 time use survey results.

This applies both to men and women who work on family farms and businesses; however, it is important to underline that in absolute terms there are fewer women involved in productive activities than men, as they are mostly busy with housework. Hence women's relative access to income-generating activities is also lower than men's, as shown in Figure 17. The few jobs that are paid, either in cash, kind, or cash and kind, are mostly carried out by men.

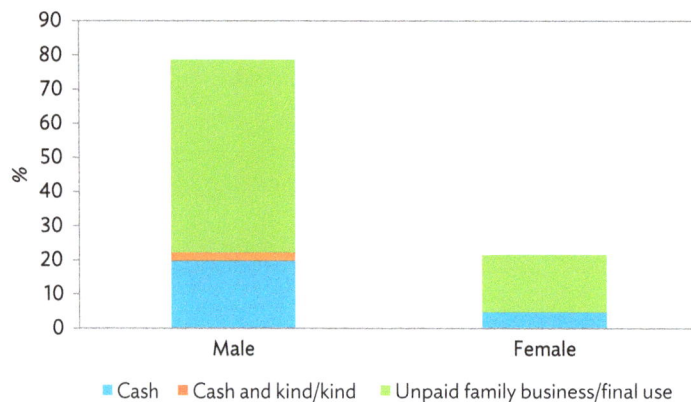

Figure 17: Type of Payment for Productive Occupations—Share of Respondents by Sex

Source: Author's computation based on 2019 time use survey results.

It also should be noted that these data refer to the main occupation of respondents, who, however, might have occasional jobs that allow them to produce some income, which can be the case for many women, as confirmed by qualitative interviews. Some women work during the harvesting season, either in their family farm or as day workers; others have small entrepreneurial activities on the side like tailoring or baking that vary in size, but usually generate very little income. Depending on the case and amount, women may consider this their own pocket money or pool it with their family.

Decisions on how to spend household income also show a clear gender divide.

As shown in Figure 18, among interviewed women, only 4.5% take decisions on income allocation independently and all these women are widowed or separated. On the other hand, 35.2% of men declared that they take such decisions autonomously, but the great majority of these men are married.

Over 20% of women declared they have no say on income allocation whatsoever, with their husbands making unilateral decisions on spending, while a smaller proportion indicated another male household member is the decision maker on household income (usually the father-in-law or brother-in-law). Among men, 6.7% declared that they have no say in decision-making in income as another male household member is in charge. No man declared that his wife takes decisions on household income without consulting him.

About half of the women who were interviewed said that they take decisions on household income with their spouse or partner, whereas men felt that joint decision-making with their wives was not as frequent (21%). One out of three men explained that these decisions are taken together with other household members, which may or may not include their wife, parents, and brothers.

Figure 18: Decision-Making on Allocation of Household Income—Share of Respondents by Sex

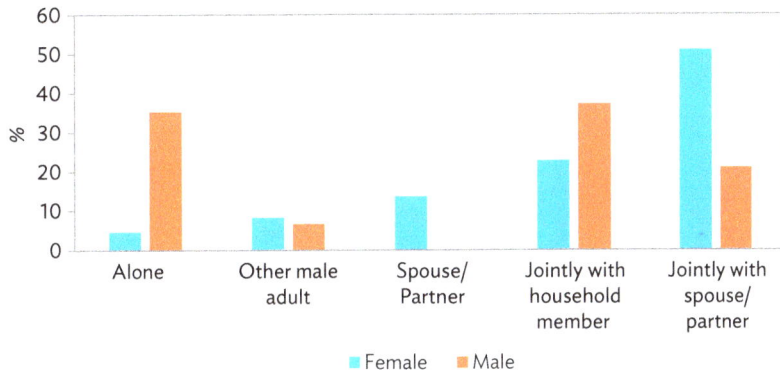

Source: Author's computation based on 2019 time use survey results.

Figure 19: Income Allocation Decision Makers—Share of Respondents

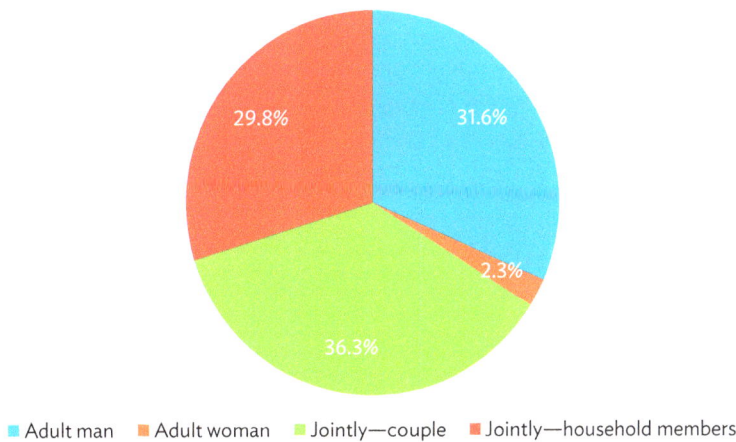

Source: Author's computation based on 2019 time use survey results.

Globally, adult women are the main decision makers only in 2.3% of the cases, and, based on survey data, all these women are all widowed or separated. Men take decisions autonomously in 31.6% of cases and decisions are taken jointly in roughly two out of three households (Figure 19).

The picture painted by the survey, where rural women have little agency and autonomy, was confirmed by qualitative interviews. However, these showed clearly that women tend to gain power in the household and the wider social sphere as they get older. When her husband dies, a woman usually becomes the head of the household, together with the oldest son, and assumes a variety of decision-making powers, including regarding allocation of income, children's education, and migration of household members. Women also are deeply respected by family members and perceived as being essential in maintaining harmony and good relations in the household.

As shown in Table 6, regarding financial inclusion, the share of women who have a bank account (25.5%) is higher than men (21.7%). This is especially true for older women and it is due to women over age 58 receiving a state pension, and, therefore, obliged to open a bank account if they do not already have one. Men instead must be at least aged 63 to receive a pension. Younger men, on the other hand, have a higher probability of having a bank account than younger women. As regards participation in saving groups, only 2% of men and no women participate in saving groups.

Table 6: Financial Inclusion
(%)

Item	Female	Male
Bank account	25.5	21.7
Savings groups	–	2.0

Source: Author's computation based on 2019 time use survey results.

Men tend to fare better than women both in terms of access to the internet and mobile phone ownership. Only 1 out of 10 women has access to the internet, while for men the proportion is one out of four (Figure 20). Almost all men (93.4%) own a mobile phone, whereas for women the percentage is 40%.

Political participation is also higher for men than for women, as shown in Figure 21. As regards water users' associations, about one out of three men participates, whereas very few women do. Figures for farmer organization participation are low for both men and women.

Qualitative interviews showed that older women that are well-off and relatively educated have higher chances of participating in community organizations and local government structures.

A married woman that was interviewed, a farmer and a landowner, had been the head of the *mahalla* (community) for a number of years, which implied dealing with diverse community issues like domestic violence and problems like electricity cuts or lack of water.

Figure 20: Share of Respondents with Access to the Internet

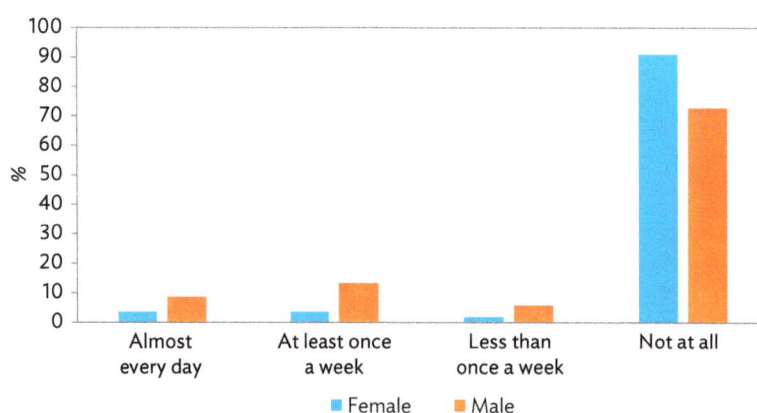

Source: Author's computation based on 2019 time use survey results.

Figure 21: Political and Social Participation

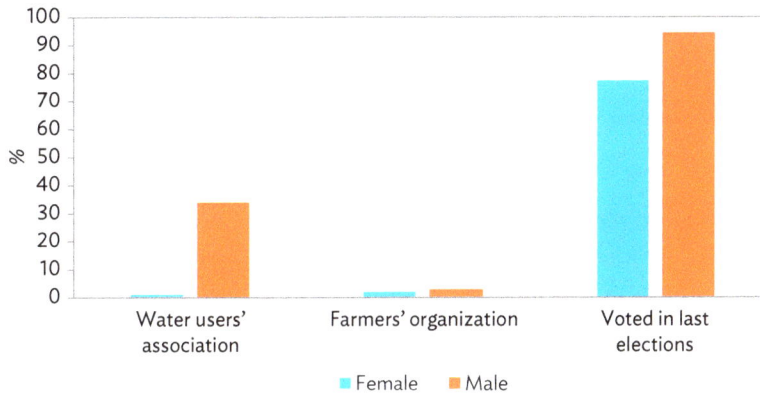

Source: Author's computation based on 2019 time use survey results.

Another married woman from Khuroson, both a teacher and a large landowner, explained that she is part of a community group that supports community members who are enduring some type of hardship. Other middle-aged, relatively educated women, mostly teachers or members of the *jamoat* (local government), also explained that they participate in community meetings and have a voice there. However, the situation of these women can in no way be considered typical and it is clearly affected by their social class, particularly their level of education, with relatively well-off women who are not educated possibly preferring not to participate in community meetings. This is the case of an older respected widowed woman from Khuroson, who heads a large household together with her older son. She explained that even though she formally is a member of the water users' association, it is her son who usually participates.

Voting in the last general elections was nearly universal for men (94%), and more than three-quarters of women also voted.

V. Gender Analysis of Time Use

The survey carried out in rural Tajikistan revealed highly gendered time use patterns: unpaid care and domestic responsibilities are overwhelmingly assigned to women—7 hours and 40 minutes for women versus 40 minutes for men—whereas paid work is mainly performed by men—5 hours and 30 minutes for men versus 1 hour and 40 minutes for women. Unpaid work for the household's final use is shared more equitably, with women doing 1 hour and 20 minutes a day versus 1 hour and 40 minutes for men.

As in most countries worldwide, rural women in Tajikistan work more than men when unpaid care and domestic work are factored in: the ratio of time that women dedicate to work compared to men is equal to 1.26. This result is in line with ratios in other countries in the region like the Kyrgyz Republic or Armenia. The excess workload of women means that they have less time available for leisure than men, almost 1 hour and 50 minutes versus 3 hours. Moreover, if time dedicated to secondary activities is factored in, women's days get longer by 2 hours and 40 minutes, mainly due to simultaneous care, compared to 40 minutes for men for extra leisure.

The analysis of the different categories of work showed that, within paid labor, the main occupation for both men and women is growing crops, particularly wheat, cotton, fruits, and vegetables. Unpaid work for the household's final use, on the other hand, is mostly aimed at farming animals and, to a lesser extent, growing crops and gathering wood. As for unpaid care and domestic work, cooking and caring for children are the most time-consuming activities, but cleaning and washing clothes also take up a good portion of women's days.

The analysis of time use patterns by sex and age groups for selected activities produced some interesting insights into the importance of age and gender as organizing factors of social and family structures in rural Tajikistan.

Young women aged 20 to 29 work the most compared to any other age group and gender. These women do 3.5 more hours of work than men in the same age group and 2.5 more hours of work than men aged 30 to 44. The gender disparity in terms of total work, however, shifts in favor of women when they enter their sixties: women who are aged 60 or older dedicate less time to work and more time to leisure and socializing than men in the same age group. These results confirmed that existing cultural norms assign elderly women a more powerful role in the household and in society.

A. Time Use Patterns

As shown in Figure 22, the gender analysis of time use patterns reveals the typical sexual division of labor. The starkest inequality has to do with the distribution of household and care responsibilities since women take these on almost completely, averaging nearly 7 hours per day versus 40 minutes for men. In terms of formal employment and other paid work a marked difference is also evident, in that

Figure 22: Time Use by Macro-Activity by Sex
(hours)

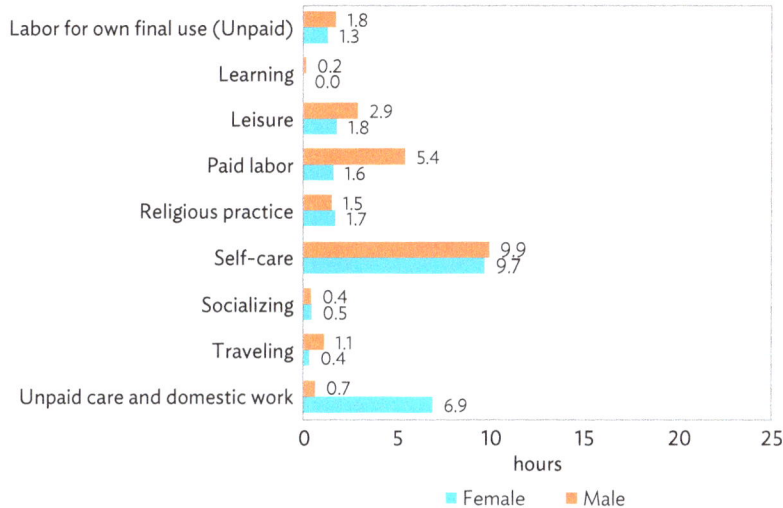

Activity	Female	Male
Labor for own final use (Unpaid)	1.3	1.8
Learning	0.0	0.2
Leisure	1.8	2.9
Paid labor	1.6	5.4
Religious practice	1.7	1.5
Self-care	9.7	9.9
Socializing	0.5	0.4
Traveling	0.4	1.1
Unpaid care and domestic work	6.9	0.7

Source: Author's computation based on 2019 time use survey results.

men dedicate to paid labor more than three times as much time as women, on average 5 hours and 30 minutes per day versus 1 hour and 40 minutes per day. The amount of labor that women and men carry out for the household's final use is much closer: 1 hour and 20 minutes for women versus 1 hour and 40 minutes for men.

As regards socializing and religious practice, in many classifications of activities that are adopted in TUSs, they belong to the same broader category of community activities, since in many societies religious practice can be a collective ritual.[46] However, in rural Tajikistan people tend to pray at home, unlike in Dushanbe or in bigger cities, where men at least go to the mosque. In Tajikistan, women do not go to the mosque at all. Hence, the religious practice category is presented and analyzed separately from socializing. On average, women spend slightly more time on religious practice than men (1 hour and 40 minutes versus 1 hour and 30 minutes, approximately) and about the same time socializing, less than 30 minutes per day. Religious practice also includes preparatory activities like washing oneself and setting out the carpet.

Leisure time, which includes watching TV or resting (the activities mostly mentioned by the respondents) is 1 hour higher on average for men than for women: while men enjoy almost 3 hours of leisure per day, women have less than 2 hours per day. This is clearly connected to the gender inequalities in terms of unpaid work just mentioned, that is, women have less time left in their day for leisure than men. As will be explained in section V-E, this also changes very much depending on the age of women and men.

Typically, self-care takes up a lot of human beings' time. This is in line with results on self-care and maintenance in rural Tajikistan, where figures show that on average men and women spend between

---

[46] See Appendix 1.

9.5 to 10 hours per day on self-care. This category includes sleeping, eating, personal hygiene, and other types of self-care like medical care.

The data also show that men's mobility is higher than women's, averaging 1 hour and 10 minutes versus approximately 20 minutes. This is understandable since, overwhelmingly, women are engaged in home-based activities. Often, traditional societal norms restrict rural women's mobility, especially younger rural women.

The distribution of time in terms of the location where the activities were undertaken is coherent with the time use patterns (Table 7). Women spend most of their time at home, on average 21 hours per day, which includes time spent sleeping and other self-care, while for men this figure is equal to 15.5 hours. Men spend over 7 hours outside of and away from the household, either doing farm work or in some other workplace, whereas for women this figure is about 2.5 hours per day. On average men also move 1 hour per day, be it in a car, walking, or with an animal (disaggregated figures will be presented in the section about travel). For women this figure is equal to 20 minutes.

Table 7: Share of Daily Time by Location and by Sex
(%)

Location	Female	Male
At home	88.5	64.9
Outside	10.0	30.3
Moving	1.5	4.8

Source: Author's computation based on 2019 time use survey results.

These time patterns are roughly in line with results found in other developing countries, especially in Asia and the Middle East. Total work (paid and unpaid) has been found to occupy about 30% of women's days in the Kyrgyz Republic, 30% in Armenia, and almost 40% in Mongolia. Figures for men are usually slightly lower in most of these countries due to lower levels of unpaid work. In rural Tajikistan, women and men spend, respectively, 41% and 33% of their day working (Figure 23). As regards self-care, it tends to occupy a lot of people's time, about 45% in the Kyrgyz Republic, 48% in Turkey, and over 50% in countries such as India, Armenia, or Mongolia. It is about 40% in rural Tajikistan.[47]

It is also worth recalling that the survey took place during October and November, hence it reflects the fall season and not the whole year. During qualitative interviews, an effort was made to enquire as to how much seasonality affects time dedicated to work and other activities. It was found that the amount of unpaid domestic and care work tends to increase in winter, but it is otherwise relatively stable. As for agricultural work, all interviewees agreed that this changes during the year: winter can be considered a much slower period, almost a time to rest from agricultural activities; in spring, work picks up and, together with summer, is the busiest period of the year, due to planting and harvesting activities. Harvest time (either summer or fall for some crops) is when all able household members tend to be involved in farm work, even women who usually aren't.

[47] J. Charmes. 2015. Time Use Across the World: Findings of a World Compilation of Time Use Surveys. Background Paper. UNDP Human Development Report Office. All the figures on time use for other countries presented in section V refer to the last available national TUS in each of the mentioned countries as reported by this study.

Figure 23: Share of Daily Time by Macro-Activity by Sex (%)

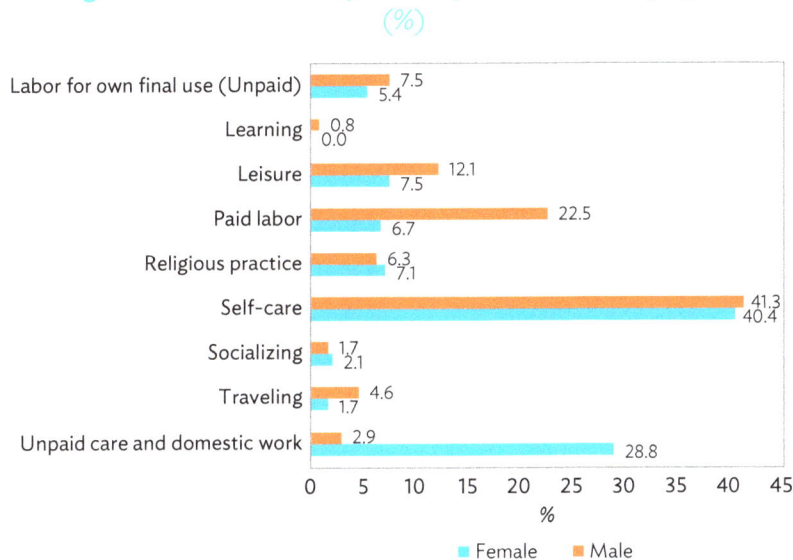

Activity	Female	Male
Labor for own final use (Unpaid)	5.4	7.5
Learning	0.0	0.8
Leisure	7.5	12.1
Paid labor	6.7	22.5
Religious practice	7.1	6.3
Self-care	40.4	41.3
Socializing	2.1	1.7
Traveling	1.7	4.6
Unpaid care and domestic work	28.8	2.9

Source: Author's computation based on 2019 time use survey results.

Simultaneous Activities

If time dedicated to simultaneous activities is added to time dedicated to the primary activity, the disparities between time use patterns of women and men deepen.

On average, a woman's day gets 2 hours and 40 minutes longer, while a man's day only get 40 minutes longer. Moreover, the time that men spend on simultaneous activities mostly corresponds to leisure time, which in most cases means watching TV while eating. In women's case, the situation is different: even though they also spend some additional time on leisure (40 minutes) when simultaneous activities are factored in, they also carry out 2 more hours of simultaneous unpaid care and domestic work. This means that they are caring for their children while working in the field or preparing lunch for field workers while washing clothes, etc. As can be seen in Figure 24, when adding up time spent on simultaneous activities, it is as if women's days were 26 hours and 40 minutes long and men's 24 hours and 40 minutes long.

Weekdays and Weekends

As could be expected, given the rural setting and the low rate of formal employment, there are no radical differences between time use patterns for weekdays and weekends, with local researchers involved in the study reporting that some respondents declared that they organized their daily activities regardless of the day of the week. However, this is not completely true, or at least not for all respondents, as the data reveal some disparities that are worth mentioning (Figures 25 and 26).

The most relevant difference between weekdays and the weekend, both for men and women, has to do with paid labor, which is on average 30 to 40 minutes less on weekends than on weekdays. Domestic and care work remains roughly the same for women, while men see an increase in the time they devote to care on weekends (from about 30 minutes to 1 hour and 15 minutes). On Sundays,

Figure 24: Time Use for Primary and Secondary Activities by Sex
(hours)

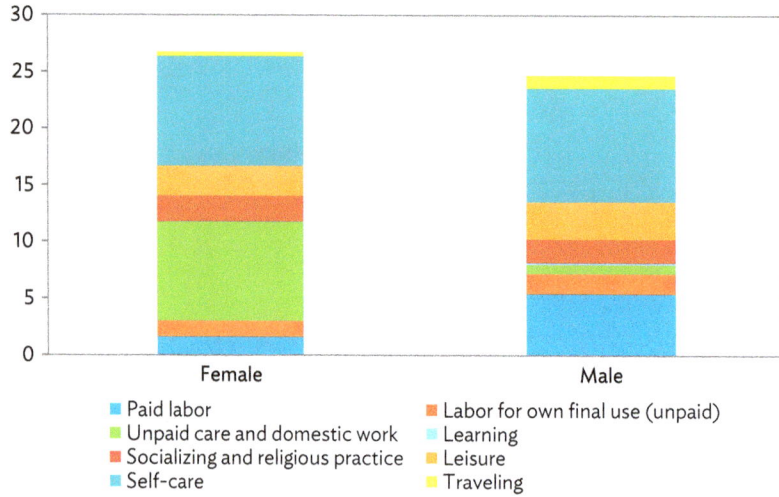

- ■ Paid labor
- ■ Labor for own final use (unpaid)
- ■ Unpaid care and domestic work
- ■ Learning
- ■ Socializing and religious practice
- ■ Leisure
- ■ Self-care
- ■ Traveling

Source: Author's computation based on 2019 time use survey results.

Figure 25: Time Use on Weekdays by Sex
(hours)

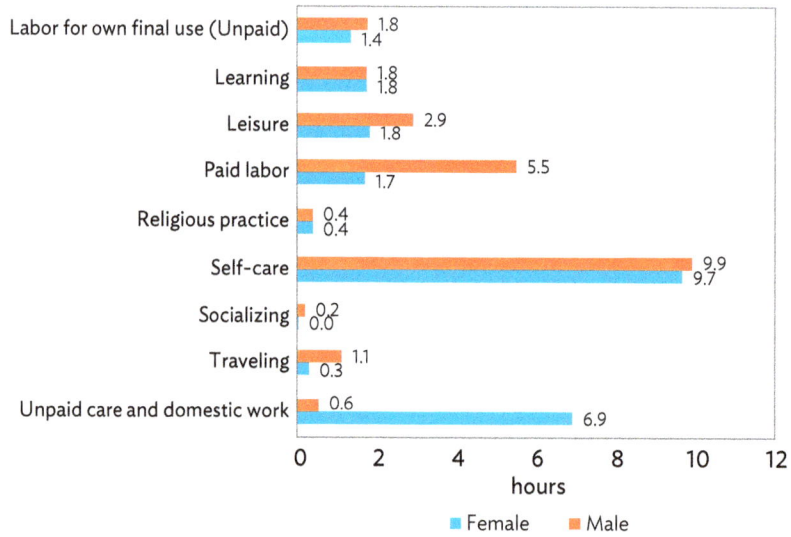

Activity	Male	Female
Labor for own final use (Unpaid)	1.8	1.4
Learning	1.8	1.8
Leisure	2.9	1.8
Paid labor	5.5	1.7
Religious practice	0.4	0.4
Self-care	9.9	9.7
Socializing	0.2	0.0
Traveling	1.1	0.3
Unpaid care and domestic work	0.6	6.9

■ Female   ■ Male

Source: Author's computation based on 2019 time use survey results.

Figure 26: Time Use on Weekends by Sex
(hours)

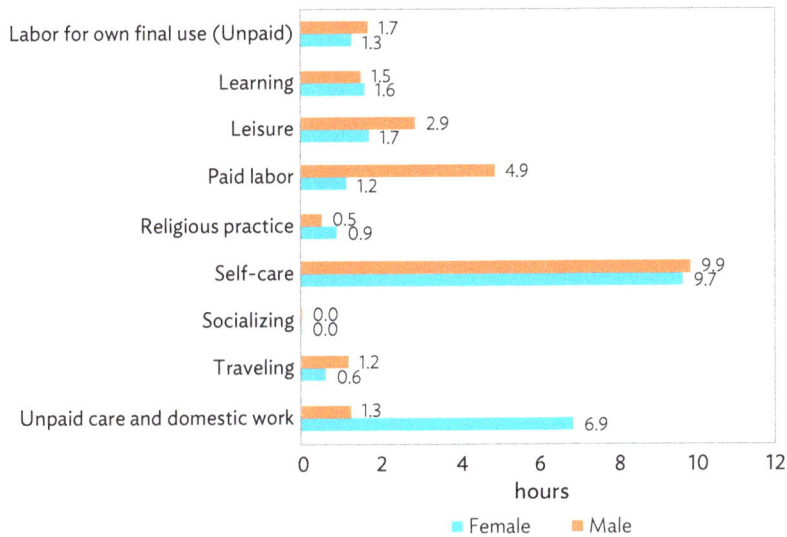

Activity	Female	Male
Labor for own final use (Unpaid)	1.3	1.7
Learning	1.6	1.5
Leisure	1.7	2.9
Paid labor	1.2	4.9
Religious practice	0.9	0.5
Self-care	9.7	9.9
Socializing	0.0	0.0
Traveling	0.6	1.2
Unpaid care and domestic work	6.9	1.3

Source: Author's computation based on 2019 time use survey results.

men spend less time working away from the household and their children are out of school; therefore, they can spend some additional time in care-related activities. Typically, care activities carried out by men include playing with children or taking them somewhere, which are considered lighter tasks within the broader category of direct and indirect care. The present TUS did not specify different types of care; a more in-depth study could investigate this.

Other relevant differences concern socializing and traveling: while for men time use in these categories barely changes on weekends, women see an increase in time spent socializing and moving, respectively by 30 minutes and 20 minutes compared to weekdays. On Sunday, women may visit their family of origin or their neighbors; to do so, they have to move, whether in the family car, with collective transport (typically common taxis), or even walking.

To sum up, even though the general time use patterns do not change much between weekdays and the weekend, both men and women spend less time in paid work, but while women spend some additional time socializing, men increase the time they devote to care. Even so, there still is a highly unequal gendered distribution of unpaid care and domestic work on Sundays.

B.   Paid and Unpaid Work

An additional meaningful indicator for revealing gender inequalities is the total time devoted to paid and unpaid work by men and women. As explained in section II, data collected through TUSs make this comparison possible by accounting for home-based and survival-related activities and providing estimates of unpaid and informal work.

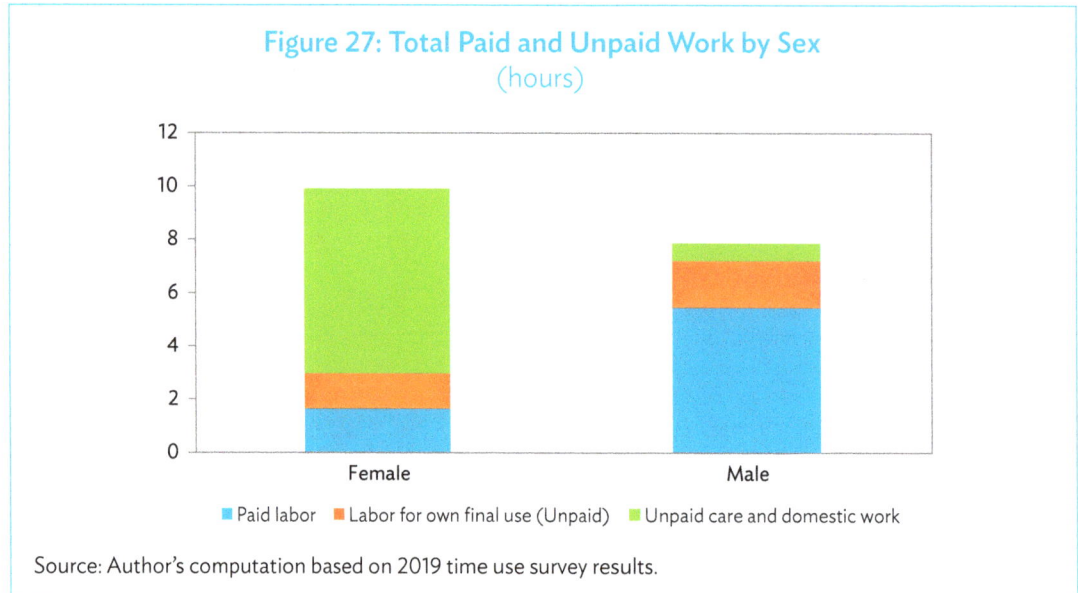

Figure 27: Total Paid and Unpaid Work by Sex
(hours)

Legend: ■ Paid labor   ■ Labor for own final use (Unpaid)   ■ Unpaid care and domestic work

Source: Author's computation based on 2019 time use survey results.

As in most countries worldwide, Tajik women work more than men when unpaid care work is factored in (Figure 27). Specifically, in rural Tajikistan women perform almost 10 hours of total work per day while men do almost 8 hours. This is in line with results for other countries in the region: in the Kyrgyz Republic, for example, women work on average 7 hours and 20 minutes while men work 6 hours; in Mongolia, women work almost 9 hours per day and men 8 hours per day; and in Armenia, women work in total 6 hours and 55 minutes and men 5 hours and 55 minutes.

It is also worth noting that there are very few countries in the world where there is parity between total work of men and women. Figures close to parity in terms of total work can be found only in a few Scandinavian countries and in some North African and Middle Eastern countries. However, while in Scandinavian countries parity in total work hours reflects an increasingly equal distribution of both paid and unpaid work, in the second group of countries parity is usually associated with an extremely low level of paid labor participation of women, that balances out with the high level of unpaid care work they perform.[48]

A more comprehensive picture of these gender inequalities is given by analyzing the relative distribution of total work in its main components: paid work, unpaid work for final use, and unpaid care and domestic work. Comparing women's and men's percentage distributions shows that while 84% of women's work is unpaid, for men this figure is equal to approximately 30%. Moreover, unpaid work performed by men is mainly for final use (22%). For women, unpaid work is mainly unpaid care and domestic work (70%), even though, as explained above, women can also be in charge of other unpaid tasks for final use (14%). As regards paid work, it constitutes almost 70% of men's total work, while it is only 16.5% for women.

These gender disparities can also be expressed though a synthetic indicator, the ratio of time that women dedicate to work compared to men, presented in Figure 28. This ratio can be calculated for any of the activities for which time use was estimated, but it is particularly meaningful when it comes to work. As can be seen in Figure 28, women's total work is 1.26 times men's; in terms of unpaid work,

---

[48] Footnote 47.

Figure 28: Number of Times That Time Spent on Work by Women Exceeds Time Spent on Work by Men

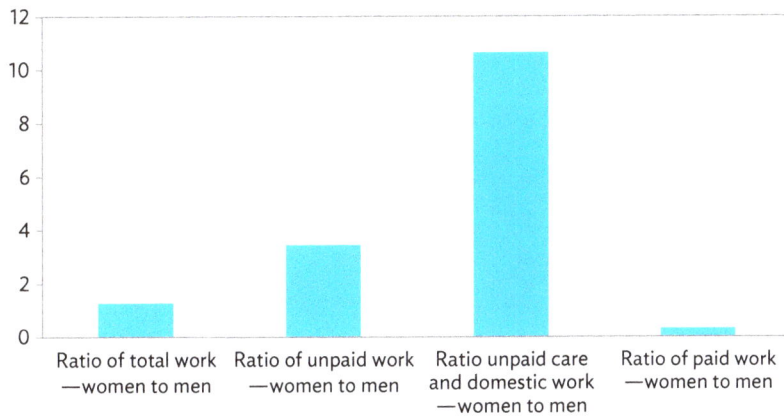

Source: Author's computation based on 2019 time use survey results.

women's time use exceeds men's by 3.4 times and if this comparison is restricted to unpaid care and domestic work only, then women do 10.6 times as much work as men. For paid work, the imbalance is inverted, as women do much less paid labor than men, the ratio being equal to 0.3.

These figures are in line with those existing for comparable Asian countries. The ratio for total work of women versus men is 1.19 in the Kyrgyz Republic, 1.17 in Armenia, and 1.04 in Pakistan. Ratios for paid work of women versus men are also in line with the results for rural Tajikistan, since in the Kyrgyz Republic it is equal to 0.61, in Armenia 0.35, and Pakistan 0.24. Unpaid work is harder to compare, as certain countries equate this to unpaid domestic care, whereas others, as in the present study (Box 1), include some household productive economic activities for final use within unpaid work, following definitions developed by feminist economists.[49]

In any case, for most Asian countries the ratio of time that women spend on unpaid work compared to men varies between 10.25 for Pakistan, 4.95 for Armenia, and 2.75 for the Kyrgyz Republic. In most developed countries, this ratio varies between 1 and 2, even though Southern Europe and Japan fare a bit worse.

In the next sections, an analysis of macro-activities and their sub-activities will be presented.

Formal Employment and Other Paid Work

Within the category employment and other paid work, both for women and men, growing wheat, cotton, and fruits and vegetables for the market takes up most of their time, about 1 hour and 4 hours per day, respectively (Figure 29). Qualitative interviews showed that there is a division of tasks based on gender, but this is not too rigid. Women tend to oversee weeding and support harvesting, and sometimes also planting. However, sodding the land or arranging for a tractor to do so, as well as trading production, are mainly men's responsibilities. It should be noted that there are some women who are heads of their farms, mainly widows, and they manage all aspects of agricultural production.

---

[49] See Hirway (2010), Razavi (2007), and Charmes (2015) for a discussion on this issue.

Figure 29: Employment and Other Work for the Market by Sex and Activity
(hours)

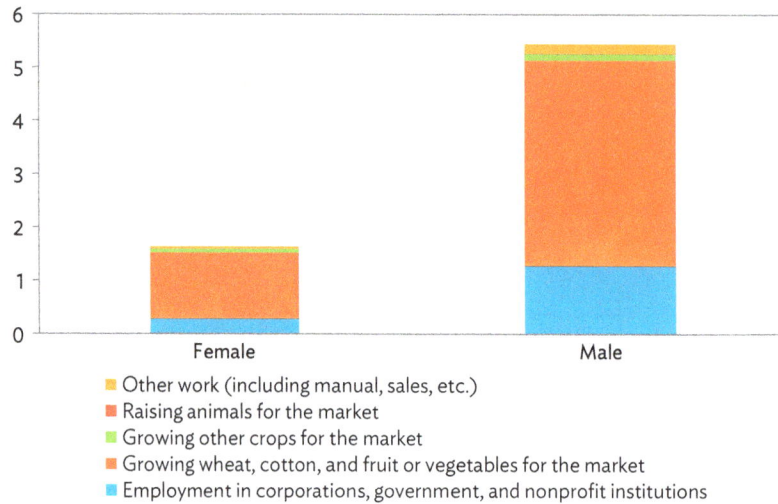

- ■ Other work (including manual, sales, etc.)
- ■ Raising animals for the market
- ■ Growing other crops for the market
- ■ Growing wheat, cotton, and fruit or vegetables for the market
- ■ Employment in corporations, government, and nonprofit institutions

Source: Author's computation based on 2019 time use survey results.

The data collected in the survey on time dedicated to paid work can also be seen to reflect the distribution of the job market in the rural setting that was studied. As explained in the methodology, work that is specifically for the family's final use is classified separately, whereas the categories "formal employment" and "other types of work done for the market" correspond to paid labor. Hence the distribution of time spent on different types of paid work should roughly reflect the structure of the labor market in the rural areas that were studied. In other words, in terms of time invested, over 72% of labor is dedicated to growing crops for the market; 22% is dedicated to employment in corporations or government, that in this area usually corresponds to a governmental institution; and about 3% of time is also dedicated to other types of work, including manual labor, handicraft, or trade.

Unpaid Labor for Own Final Use

As shown in Figure 30, men and women respectively dedicate to labor for own final use approximately 1 hour and 30 minutes and 1 hour and 20 minutes per day, respectively. Within this category farming animals takes up most time both for women (43 minutes) and men (52 minutes), followed by growing crops and gathering firewood.

According to the survey, about 90% of households have farm animals. As previously mentioned, in growing and managing animals, men and women have different tasks and usually care for different animals. The survey did not capture this specificity; however, the qualitative interviews showed that usually women oversee the poultry and milking cows and cleaning the stall in the household. Men, by contrast, oversee the bigger livestock, including access to veterinary services, trade, and grazing the animals or arranging for someone to help with grazing.

Gathering wood is a shared responsibility, as, on average, men and women dedicate from 10 to 15 minutes per day to this task. This was also confirmed by qualitative interviews and direct observation: twigs and wood are gathered at the end of the cotton harvest as well as in November

Figure 30: Labor for Own Final Use by Activity and Sex
(hours)

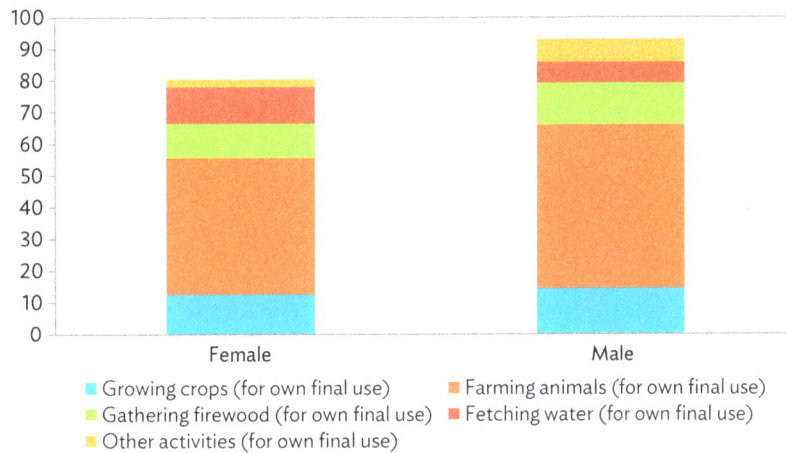

Source: Author's computation based on 2019 time use survey results.

and December before winter starts. This is one of the cases where seasonality of this survey should be considered, as data were collected in the months of October and November when wood gathering is necessary. During the harvest season, for example, people are busy with other tasks and time dedicated to wood gathering will probably be less as it is not necessary for heating in the summer. However, some wood is still used for cooking and will need to be gathered.

Fetching water is more often a task for women and older children. When men are involved in collecting water, this is usually only to agree on the price and delivery of water by trucks. Actual fetching of water for household needs is mostly women's responsibility.

Unpaid Domestic and Care Work

As detailed above, women take up most of the domestic and care work in the household. Within this category, cooking (2 hours and 15 minutes), caring for children (2 hours and 12 minutes), cleaning and tidying up (1 hour and 12 minutes), and washing clothes (1 hour) take up most of women's time (Figure 31). Men's time within this category is mostly spent caring for children (about 40%).

If compared with time use statistics on direct and indirect care in other countries of the region, the figures for rural Tajikistan are quite high. In the Kyrgyz Republic (rural and urban), women spend 20 minutes per day caring for children and about 4 hours per day in other domestic services; in Pakistan, figures are approximately 1 hour for domestic work and 4 hours for direct care.[50]

The amount of time that women put into care and domestic activities in rural Tajikistan has to do in the first place with the high degree of gender inequality of its distribution: women do 92% of the work and men only do the remaining 8%. Direct and indirect care are highly concentrated

---

[50] J. Charmes. 2015. *Time Use Across the World: Findings of a World Compilation of Time Use Surveys*. Background Paper. UNDP Human Development Report Office.

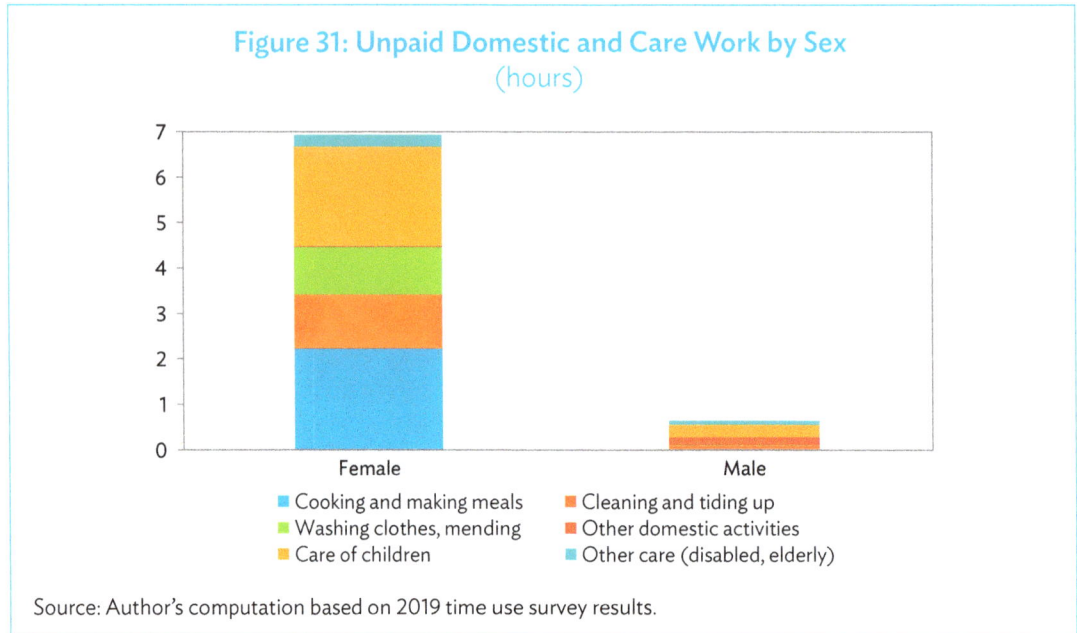

Figure 31: Unpaid Domestic and Care Work by Sex
(hours)

Legend:
- Cooking and making meals
- Cleaning and tiding up
- Washing clothes, mending
- Other domestic activities
- Care of children
- Other care (disabled, elderly)

Source: Author's computation based on 2019 time use survey results.

in women's hands, who find themselves running large rural households that require a lot of emotional and manual labor.

The emotional labor of direct care has to do mainly with children and possibly disabled or dependent family members. In this respect, a factor affecting women's workload is the size of rural households and particularly the number of children. On average, there are four children and six adults in each household, possibly including disabled or elderly family members and migrant members who are temporarily abroad. In households where there are members with a disability or dependent adults, there also tends to be more care work for women, on average 40 minutes more than in households where there are no dependent adults.

As regards manual labor inherent in domestic services, this is clearly affected by the characteristics of the dwelling that rural families live in. Families usually live in a detached house or in several small detached houses opening on the same common yard, with an outdoor latrine, a home garden, and a stall for farm animals. Cooking and making meals, which takes up most of women's unpaid work, is often done with wood (55% of households use wood at least sometimes) or animal dung (12%). Clothes are washed by hand in the great majority of households (75%). Keeping up the so-called reproduction of families in these dwellings obviously requires a great deal of work, even though the housing conditions themselves are relatively good as roofs and walls are mostly finished and access to electricity is nearly universal.

It is worth noting that using traditional fuels increases the amount of time spent cooking. In households where wood or animal dung are the main fuel, women cook from 2.5 to 3 hours a day, compared to 1.5 hours for gas and 2 hours for electricity.

In addition, having access to a washing machine reduces the time women spend washing clothes by 30%, owning a vacuum cleaner (13.9%) and a refrigerator (84.7%) have no clear effect on domestic work.

C.   Leisure, Personal Reproduction Functions, and Social Activities

Activities like self-care, as well as learning, leisure, or rest, can be thought of as serving personal reproduction and being included in what some scholars call the person system.[51] If this is obvious for activities like sleeping or eating, by extension studying or leisure also serve self-reproduction, or, in other words, the formation of human capital. Since praying is also mostly a private activity in rural Tajikistan, it can be included within the personal functions group.

Socializing and community activities include socializing with relatives and the community at large, as well as political and social participation broadly speaking.

As shown in Figure 32, interestingly the total time for self-care for men and women is practically the same, almost 10 hours per day, of which about 6 hours and 40 minutes to sleep; 2 hours and 20 minutes approximately for eating; and the rest for other types of self-care, including hygiene and medical care. This is in line with results in the region, as human beings tend to have a standard amount of time they spend for self-maintenance: in Armenia, the Kyrgyz Republic, Mongolia, and Pakistan, time for self-care varies from 10 to 12 hours per day.

There are no relevant gender inequalities for religious practice, either, as both men and women pray on average 1 hour and 30 minutes to 1 hour and 40 minutes per day.

The only personal activity that shows a meaningful gender disparity is leisure, which includes watching TV, resting, or reading: men enjoy almost 3 hours of leisure per day, while women have about 1 hour and 45 minutes. The lower availability of leisure time for women is clearly a consequence of their excess work.

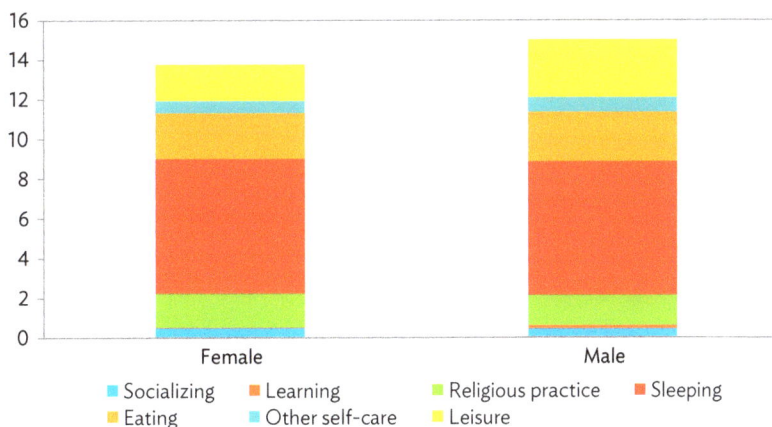

Figure 32: Leisure, Self-Care, and Other Personal Reproduction Functions (hours)

Source: Author's computation based on 2019 time use survey results.

[51] S. Singh et al. 2010. Local Studies Manual: A Researcher's Guide for Investigating the Social Metabolism of Rural Systems. *Working Paper*. No. 120. Vienna: Institute for Social Ecology.

There also is a disparity in terms of time dedicated to learning, which is on average 10 minutes per day for men and close to zero for women. It should be noted that these figures are based on a very small number of people who declared they spent at least some of their time learning; hence, the difference is not as significant. In general, both the adult men and women in the studied area dedicate very little time to learning and studying, including training.[52]

Time dedicated to socializing and other community activities is pretty much the same for men and women. As previously noted, it increases a bit for women on Sundays. This category also includes communal work and while qualitative interviews showed that in rural Tajikistan there are some communal work activities, these are quite hard to capture with a one-off pilot time use study (TUS). It is worth noting, however, that one of the men that was interviewed referred to a communal grazing practice that worked by sharing the responsibility of grazing the livestock of all the community members: each member of this group is in charge of grazing a few days per month.

D.   Travel

Time dedicated daily to travel by women is much more limited than time dedicated by men, averaging approximately 20 minutes versus 1 hour and 10 minutes. The lower mobility of women has to do with their main occupation being domestic work that doesn't require travel and with restrictions that are imposed especially on younger women due to traditional patriarchal norms. Qualitative interviews revealed that women do not see the quality of road infrastructure or safety as problems limiting their movements. Many women declared that, depending on the family, a woman can have more or fewer restrictions on moving. Nearly all, except for older women, declared that they ask their husband and mother-in-law for permission to go and that they are usually accompanied by other family members. Some mentioned the cost of public transport as a restrictive factor in traveling. The distribution of total travel time by mode of transportation is presented in Figure 33.

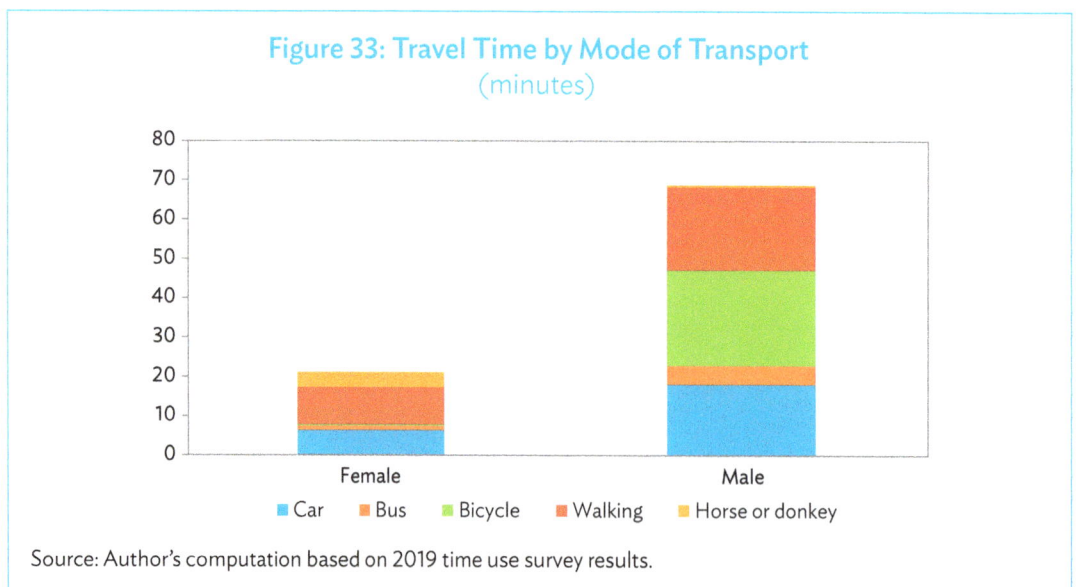

Figure 33: Travel Time by Mode of Transport
(minutes)

Source: Author's computation based on 2019 time use survey results.

---

[52] It is worth recalling that only persons who are aged 20 or older were eligible to participate in this survey.

Men's most-used mode of transport is the bicycle (24 minutes), followed by walking (21 minutes), and the car (18 minutes). For women, the most common way to move is walking (10 minutes) followed by the car (6 minutes) and animal traction (4 minutes). It should be noted that 55.6% of households own a car, 75% own a bicycle, and only 1.4% own a motorbike (Table 4). Collective taxis are widespread in rural Tajikistan so respondents mentioning car as a means of transportation are not necessarily referring to their own private care.

E.   Time Use Patterns by Age Group

The analysis of time patterns by sex and age groups for selected activities (Figure 34) gives some interesting insights into the importance of age and gender as organizing factors of social and family structures.

Women dedicate most time to work when they are young: from age 20 to 29, women work on average 11 hours and 10 minutes per day, including paid and unpaid work. This remains relatively stable, though diminishing a bit, when women are in their 30s and early 40s. It decreases more visibly for the 45–59 age group and nearly half for women who are aged 60 or older (5 hours and 50 minutes).

As regards the different types of work undertaken, some observations follow.

The peak of unpaid domestic and care work for women (8 hours and 10 minutes) is when they are youngest (age 20 to 29), as this is when smaller and more time-consuming children are usually part of the household. This is also when women are at the lowest level of power in the household. As mentioned, in rural Tajikistan, it is overwhelmingly the case for newlywed women to move into their husband's household and live with their parents-in-law and possibly brothers- and sisters-in-law's families. These young women, as also observed during qualitative interviews, are the ones who run the household while taking care of the children.

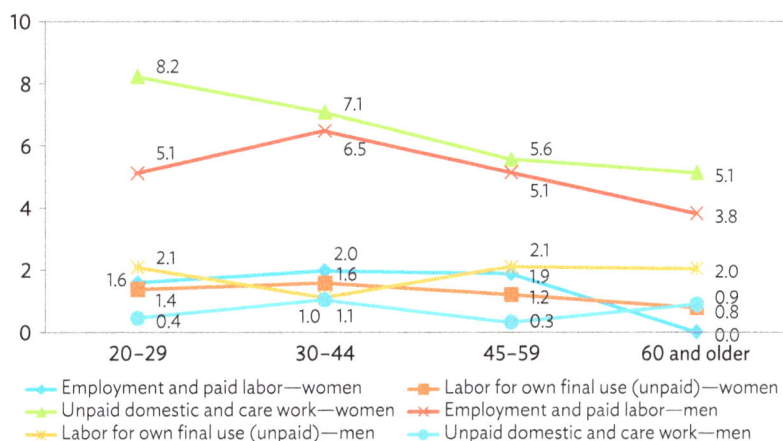

Figure 34: Paid and Unpaid Work by Age Group and by Sex
(hours)

Source: Author's computation based on 2019 time use survey results.

Time for unpaid care work diminishes with age, but remains significant for all age groups. Even women in their 60s and older have many household responsibilities, about 5 hours per day, but qualitative interviews showed that these tend to shift toward household management tasks, care of grandchildren, and other emotional care tasks. Not only do elderly women assign tasks to household members, they also are the guarantors of peace and good family relations. As many reported, "my mother[-in-law] controls everyone and guarantees harmony in the household."

The other unpaid labor that rural women carry out, which, as mentioned above, corresponds mainly to farming animals and growing crops in the home garden, does not vary very much with age, even though there is a peak in the 30–44 age group (about 1 hour and 35 minutes) and it decreases for women over age 60.

Time dedicated to formal employment and other paid work also peaks when women are in their 30s and early 40s, as by then women usually have slightly older children and can dedicate increasingly more time to work that is not care work. According to qualitative interviews, when a woman gives birth, she is not involved in farm work for 1 or even 2 years, depending on the family. While all types of work decrease for women aged 60 or older, time dedicated to paid labor becomes equal to zero. It should be noted that the pension age in Tajikistan is 58 for women and 63 for men; hence, women over 58 are not engaged in any formal employment or paid labor. However, it might be the case that some women over age 60 do some paid work and that they are reticent to declare this as receiving a pension from the state does not allow them to work.

Men's situation is somewhat different. The peak in terms of men's total work (8 hours and 40 minutes) comes when they are between 30 and 44 years old, with total work slowly decreasing thereafter. Men in their 60s or older still work over 6 hours a day.

Since paid labor is the main component of total work, the peak for time dedicated to it (about 6.5 hours) is also when men are in their 30s and early 40s. Subsequently paid labor decreases slowly, with men aged 60 and older doing about 3 hours and 50 minutes of paid work per day.

Unpaid work as a whole goes from 2.5 hours in the 20 to 29 age group to 3 hours for men aged 60 and older. It does, however, shrink somewhat for men between ages 30 and 44, when men are doing more paid work, which in most societies is typical of the central stages of the life cycle. Men in their 30s and early 40s in fact will mostly have a family of their own, even though they might be living in their parents' households, and will be in need of paid work to support their family. As previously mentioned, households have on average 10 members, of which 4 are children, while men's average age at marriage is 24.[53]

As regards the time that women dedicate to leisure, religious practice, and socializing, it increases steadily for all categories with age (Figure 35). As could be expected, given the results on paid and unpaid work presented above, time for leisure, socializing, and even praying (though to a lesser extent) is scarcest for younger women and highest for older women. As several younger women who were interviewed reported, with small children, housework, and helping out in the fields, there is no spare time at all for leisure (see Parvina's story in section VI-B).

Time for leisure in particular goes from 1 hour and 15 minutes on average for younger women to 3 hours and 45 minutes for elder women, whereas socializing only occupies 20 minutes daily for younger

---

[53] Fertility rate per woman for Khatlon according to last Demographic and Health Survey (TSI, 2017) is 4.1.

Figure 35: Leisure, Socializing, and Religious Practice by Sex
(hours)

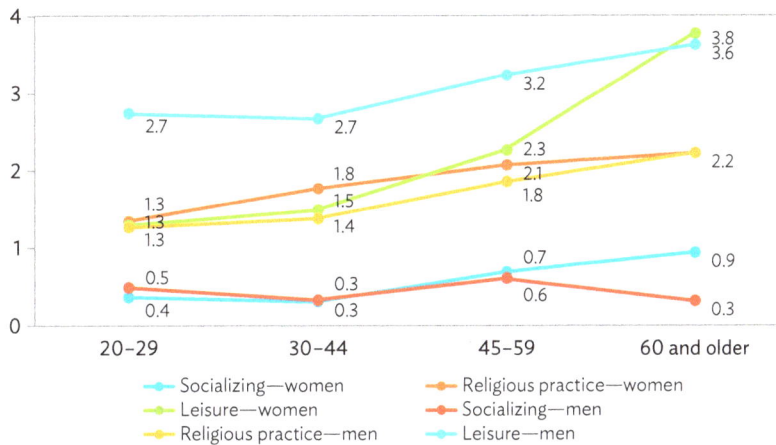

Source: Author's computation based on 2019 time use survey results.

women and reaches 1 hour for women in their 60s or older. As for religious practice, the increase is less dramatic, from 1 hour and 20 minutes to over 2 hours.

The figures for the time that men dedicate to leisure, religious practice, and socializing also reflect the results on paid and unpaid work presented above. Men have slightly less time for leisure and socializing in their 30s and early 40s than in their 20s (3 hours versus 3 hours and 10 minutes) while praying time is more or less the same (about 1 hour and 15 minutes). The time dedicated to all these activities, however, grows in the later stages of life, reaching over 6 hours in total for older men: 2 hours and 10 minutes of religious practice, 3 hours and 40 minutes of leisure and 20 minutes of socializing.

To sum up, several observations can be made on the compared time patterns of women and men by age group.

Young women, aged 20 to 29, are the ones who work the most. These women do 3.5 more hours of work than men in the same age group and 2.5 more hours of work than men aged 30 to 44. As for leisure, young women have half as much leisure time than men of the same age: 1 hour and 20 minutes versus 2 hours and 40 minutes.

The figures for persons in the younger age groups are clearly also affected by social institutions like marriage that tend to happen earlier for women than for men. On average, women in our sample get married at age 19 and men at age 24. This means that some of the men in the 20 to 29 group are not married yet, which clearly affects lifestyle and time use, especially compared to women of the same age group who will mostly be married.

The gender disparity in terms of total work shifts in favor of women when they enter their 60s: women who are aged 60 or older dedicate less time to work (5 hours and 55 minutes) than men in the same age group (6 hours and 40 minutes). Even though the difference is substantial, it is still quite low compared to the number of additional hours of work carried out by women in other phases of their life.

As for time dedicated to leisure, women aged 60 and older enjoy more time for leisure and socializing: 4 hours and 40 minutes for women versus 4 hours for men. It can also be noted that existing cultural norms assign elderly women a more powerful role in the household and in society, as emerged clearly in qualitative interviews. Often these older women, especially after their husband dies, become the head of the household together with their oldest son.

Interestingly, time dedicated by men to religion in the different life stages is quite similar to time dedicated to it by women and exactly the same when they enter their 60s (2 hours and 10 minutes).

VI. Rural Women and Intra-Household Relations

The following stories were selected from the qualitative in-depth interviews that were carried out in rural households in the targeted districts after the time use study (TUS) was implemented. They confirm and enrich the results of the survey, adding details on the general structure and gendered organization of households and work.

A.   Household 1

Household 1 is in Khuroson district. It is composed of a grandmother aged 71, her daughter, and two of her married sons with their wives and children. Her husband died a few years ago. He was an agronomist in the local government. He could not own land, which is why the certificate was placed under her name. This family used to have a big plot of land (25 hectares), a *dekhan* farm (private smallholder farm), but they returned part of it to the government as it was no longer profitable due to of lack of irrigation and taxes.[54] They now only work on 3 hectares of land. The man had accumulated a big debt over the years, as he was not able to repay the loans he used to buy agricultural inputs and pay taxes. His family considers his death a direct consequence of these debts.

Box 2: Interviewee 1

She is one of the daughters-in-law in Household 1; she is 46 years old and has 6 children. She oversees domestic and care activities, while her husband works on the farm and occasionally does manual work (e.g., construction and repair). The extended family living in this household is quite large and all the women help with care work and domestic chores.

She would have liked to get a job, but her parents didn't let her get an education and married her off when she was 17. She did not know her husband when she got married. Besides doing housework, she works on the family farm or for other landowners when she gets the chance. Particularly in autumn she is hired with some of her neighbors for the cotton harvest. She usually gets about TJS15 a day for this and it is the only chance she has to earn money for herself.

Her decision-making power in the household is very limited. All decisions on income are taken by her husband and her mother-in-law; she only leaves the household to work on the land or for specific events, but always with the approval of her husband and mother-in-law.

Source: Author's interview with respondent from Khuroson on 13 December 2019.

---

[54] As explained above, in Tajikistan, access to land has a specific legal meaning, i.e., there is really no private land ownership, but individuals have the right to use land through land tenure agreements with the government. However, in line with other studies on the subject, in this report, ownership of land is understood as the right to use land conveyed to individuals whose names are included on land certificates and licenses.

Box 3: Interviewee 2

She is the elderly woman's daughter. She was married, but her husband rejected her as they were not able to have children and he went to the Russian Federation to work. She used to live with her husband's family, but after separating she moved back with her mother. Her mother-in-law rejected her as well because she considered her disabled, as she did not have children. She was the third wife of this man and he had never had children before. She was married for 4 years and does not want to divorce. She and her husband are still occasionally in touch over the phone and he still exercises control over her. Even after they separated, he was violent with her when she attended a wedding without his consent. She does domestic work, but does not help on the farm. She does not leave the house and has no interest in taking training courses, doing agricultural work, or learning some other skills. This young woman has suffered a lot of pressure and social stigma for not having children. Even though she has no control over her ability to get pregnant, she was rejected by her husband and his family. Her story also points at the widespread social acceptance of violence against women.

Her own mother, however, is ashamed and surprised by her daughter's situation: "I never experienced violence with my husband... we cooked together... we did everything together..."

Source: Author's interview with respondent from Khuroson on 13 December 2019.

B.   Household 2

Household 2 is composed of Interviewee 3, her husband and children in the district of Jaihun. Her husband's parents died, so she lives with her nuclear family only. Her brother-in-law, his wife, and children live in Dushanbe and comes to Jaihun to stay during summer.

Box 4: Interviewee 3

She is in her early 30s and she has five children between the ages of 2 and 9. Her husband works as a paid worker in a dekhan farm, spraying plants, harvesting crops, and carrying out other farm work. She and her husband also grow farm animals and sell meat. She is totally in charge of caring for their children.

She only works at home, and takes care of the household farm's 15 bulls and about 40 chickens. They sell the cattle, and her husband is charge of sales, but they also sell the meat directly. She used to work in a farm, but after the birth of her third child she started having some health issues, so she stopped. It would have been hard for her to still work as she has five children and does not live in an extended family, so she has no help for childcare and housework. "I never rest because there is no time. I have five children. I don't even have time to watch TV. I have to do the housekeeping, take care of the animals. And I have five children."

Her story exemplifies the type of pressure that younger rural women can be under, as well as the time poverty they experience. It also points at the structure of the care economy in rural Tajikistan that almost totally relies on families. Where the support of the extended family is not present, as in this case, women are subject to a great deal of time stress.

continued on next page

Box 4   *continued*

Her husband takes all the decisions in the household, including on income allocation. They have been married for 13 years; before getting married she used to go to the market but now she only goes out with her husband's permission. She also asked him for permission to participate in the interview. She does not participate in meetings and other public events in the village.

Source: Author's interview with respondent from Khuroson on 13 December 2019.

C.   Household 3

Household 3 is based in the district of Khuroson. The household is made up of an elderly widowed woman and the families of three of her sons. The household has access to agricultural land (16-hectare dekhan farm) and all the adult household members are mainly occupied in agricultural or domestic activities, except for the eldest son who has a formal job in the district registry office. This household is relatively well-off within the rural world in which it is immersed, as it owns land and livestock and both the elder woman and her son have a monthly income, respectively, a pension and a government job. It is, however, a very big household and living conditions and characteristics of the dwelling are in line with most rural households in the area. The stories below outline clearly the typical organization of tasks in rural families, including paid labor, unpaid work for final use, and care and domestic work.

Box 5: Interviewee 4

She is 46 years old and married to the eldest man in the family. Her main activities are domestic and care work. She explained that domestic work is only carried out by women, while men do all the work outside of the house, including agricultural labor and repair and maintenance activities of the dwelling.

The family is big so the women clean every day, bake bread every other day, warm water for washing when they get up they, heat the stove for house heating, prepare breakfast, prepare children for school, prepare lunch, milk the cows, take care of some of the animals, and a few times a week they wash clothes.

Men are mainly occupied in productive activities, like buying necessary products for the household and the farm, paying for utilities, and doing farm work. Water at the household is either collected from the rain or bought from a truck; her husband arranges for purchase and delivery of water.

As for fuel, she and her sisters-in-law oversee making briquettes from cow dung. Firewood is mainly collected after harvesting cotton in autumn; both men and women participate.

As for care of her children, she is mainly in charge of her children's education and health in cooperation with her husband.

This is a relatively egalitarian family where, "there is an atmosphere of mutual understanding...thanks to the mother-in-law who always controls everyone." She shows a great deal of respect for the elder woman.

continued on next page

Box 5   *continued*

Agricultural labor is the responsibility of both men and women in this household, but men are in charge and also spend more time on actual fieldwork, i.e., plowing the land, hiring a tractor when needed, buying fertilizers and seeds, watering the land, and collecting and selling the crops. Women are in charge of weeding, cleaning the wheat after it is harvested, and preparing food for the tractor drivers and the men working on the land while plowing.

As for livestock, the interviewee takes care of the turkeys while her brother-in-law and son take care of the cows and sheep, especially for grazing. The women, however, milk the cows and clean the stalls.

As for autonomy and decision-making, the interviewee is one of the older women in a relatively liberal household; hence, she has more freedom of movement than other rural women. She informs her mother-in-law and husband if she leaves the house and only goes to the market with her daughter and mother-in-law. She can, however, attend meetings at her children's school if needed and would be able to participate in training courses if she wanted.

In terms of decision-making on the allocation of income, her mother-in-law and husband have the last word, but generally she also participates in discussions, as do her brothers-in-law. If she needs something, she usually has the freedom to buy it, but must consult with her husband and mother-in-law.

It is also worth noting that from 2007 to 2009 her husband was living in the Russian Federation as a migrant worker and was sending back good remittances. At that time, her father-in-law was still alive and was managing household income and taking decisions on its allocation.

Source: Author's interview with respondent from Khuroson on 12 December 2019.

Box 6: Interviewee 5

He is one of the younger adult men of the family (aged 32). He is married and has two small children. His main occupation is working on the farm, taking care of the livestock, and repairing and maintaining the dwelling. He recognizes that his older brother is his mother's right hand in managing the household.

As regards the organization of farm work, his older brother manages the farm: he gives instructions and he and his other brother do the manual work, sometimes with helpers. In autumn, they collect cotton, then they clean the land from weeds and prepare it for sowing wheat. In winter they sow wheat. After that they have time to relax from farm work. In spring and summer, the hard work starts again. In spring, they fertilize the land with fertilizers and sow cotton. In summer, they harvest wheat and grow cotton.

"Since there are problems with irrigation, the harvest is very limited... but we keep part of the harvest for our family and we sell part."

The management of bigger livestock (sheep, goats, cows) is his and his brother's responsibility. They also are helped by their neighbor, a shepherd. Livestock is sold when money is needed, for example, for food in the winter, for weddings, for repairs on the house, or for food for the livestock.

As regards his mobility, he has restrictions imposed by the cost of traveling. However, he leaves the house to work on the land or for grazing animals. He attends the mahalla (community) meetings and all the celebrations and funerals of neighbors. He also goes to the market or to the village shop if necessary. His wife never walks or leaves alone.

Decision-making is mainly up to his older brother and his mother. He must consult with them if he needs money, as he has no cash.

He worked in the Russian Federation for 6 months in 2008, but he returned to Tajikistan after breaking his leg. The money he and his brothers were able to send during that period made it possible for him to get married, buy cattle, and do some home improvements.

Source: Author's interview with respondent from Khuroson on 12 December 2019.

VII. Conclusions and Recommendations

Women in rural Tajikistan occupy a particularly disempowered position. In the last national development strategy, the government pointed out that inequality in opportunities is especially high for rural women, not only because of higher gender stereotypes and limited choices in the area of employment, but also due to a relatively low availability and quality of infrastructure, which affects access to resources and opportunities.

This study aimed at uncovering unequal gender relations in two rural districts in Tajikistan and the specific constraints that women face in different areas and phases of their life. Using time use data, the study detailed existing gender disparities in terms of paid and unpaid work, focusing on unpaid care and domestic work.

A. Main Findings

Tajik rural households are typically made up of extended multigenerational families. When women get married, they usually move into their husband's household, with his parents, siblings, and possibly siblings' families. Emigration, especially labor migration of men to the Russian Federation, is a massive phenomenon and in most households, there is at least one migrant family member working abroad or there has been one in the recent past.

Most rural families live in a detached house or in several small houses opening on the same common yard, with an outdoor latrine, a home garden, and a stall for farm animals. Access to water is somewhat problematic and many rural households either buy water or they collect it from irrigation canals and public pipes. Rainwater is also used as a secondary water source. Traditional fuels like wood and animal dung are often used for cooking and only one out of four households has a washing machine. Nearly all households own a TV, but only one every seven has access to the internet, mainly through someone's mobile.

Most households have at least two different sources of livelihood, which can include agriculture, pensions, and remittances, as well as other forms of employment. Agriculture is the main source of livelihood for most families, even though the income that it generates is very low. Households produce a variety of crops, including cotton, wheat, vegetables and fruit, both for the market and their own final use.

A deep gender divide exists in terms of economic empowerment and most rural women are in a vulnerable and disempowered position. Opportunities to participate in the paid economy are very limited and only a small minority of women are the primary owners of agricultural land and housing.

The gender analysis of time use data showed a clear gender-based division of labor, with women specializing in care and domestic activities and men specializing in productive work. The degree of specialization encountered was quite high, since for women unpaid care and domestic work represents over 70% of total work, while for men roughly the same percentage is spent in paid work.

On the one hand, men specialize in paid labor, whether formally employed or not: they take up 75% of available paid labor in terms of hours worked.[55] Women are left with the remaining 25% of the job market. As mentioned above, in developing countries, which typically have big informal sectors that are hard to capture, time use studies (TUSs) provide a valuable alternative or complement to labor force surveys. In rural Tajikistan, where formal jobs are few and most income opportunities come from the agricultural sector, the data collected in the TUS reveal that three-quarters of the labor force is employed formally or informally in the agricultural sector and about 22% is employed in corporations, government, and non-profits (i.e., formal jobs by definition). The remaining 3% is engaged in other types of jobs, including construction, sales, and handcraft. The general structure of the job market for men and women varies very little, except for the formal employment sector shrinking even more for women.

On the other hand, women specialize in unpaid labor, which includes final use and unpaid domestic and care work. As regards final use, it emerged that men carry out slightly more work than women (1 hour and 30 minutes per day versus 1 hour and 20 minutes). While there is a stark gender disparity in terms of the access to paid work for the market, the time data show that women are well represented in unpaid farm work for the household, which is associated with survival rather than income generation.

In terms of direct and indirect care, women do 10 times more work than men, almost 7 hours a day. The large workload of women is explained by the high degree of gender specialization of these activities, since in terms of hours worked, direct and indirect care are almost totally the responsibility of women (92%) and they barely concern men (8%). The total amount of work that is necessary to guarantee the survival and reproduction of families also has to do with the characteristics of the households, in terms of size of families, type of dwelling, available assets, and so on. Women, especially young ones, find themselves running large rural households that require a great deal of emotional and manual labor.

Direct care and emotional labor mainly concern children and disabled or dependent family members: on average, in each household, there are four children and six adults, possibly including disabled or elderly family members, and migrant members who are temporarily abroad. The data showed that the presence of persons with disabilities in a household increases women's workload. With respect to the manual labor associated to domestic services, cooking and making meals takes up most of women's unpaid work time and it is often done with traditional fuels, occupying over 2 hours of a woman's day. Washing clothes, tidying up, and cleaning the house account for most of the remaining domestic work.

As in most countries worldwide, when both unpaid and paid labor are considered, rural women work longer hours than men in Tajikistan. On average, women work almost 10 hours a day, as opposed to 8 hours for men. If secondary activities are factored in, the gap widens, as an additional 2 hours of simultaneous domestic and care work of women have to be accounted for.

---

[55] It should be recalled that the term "paid labor" refers to productive activities and does not necessarily imply receiving a payment. It may include work done on the family farm for which there are no profits or for which profits are managed by someone else. Definitions used here are presented in Box 1. For a discussion on what constitutes paid and unpaid labor, see Charmes (2015: 13).

Time dedicated to socializing and other community activities is much the same for men and women; however, more leisure is available to men than to women, 2 hours and 55 minutes versus 1 hour and 45 minutes, because of women's excessive workload and time poverty. As regards travel, women move much less than men, averaging approximately 20 minutes a day versus 1 hour and 10 minutes. This is in line with the main occupation of women taking place in the domestic sphere, but it also has to do with restrictions on mobility that are imposed on women, especially younger ones, due to traditional patriarchal norms.

The study revealed that age is also a very important factor in shaping cultural norms in rural Tajikistan. The analysis of gendered time patterns by age group, as well as decision-making on household income allocation, showed this clearly.

In terms of total work, both paid and unpaid, young women work more than any other age group and gender, approximately 11 hours per day. This is when smaller and more time-consuming children are usually part of the family, and also when women are at the lowest level of power in the household. For men, the peak in terms of total work comes when they are in their 30s and early 40s, when they usually are already married and have families. It is worth recalling that on average women marry younger than men, and, in most cases, newlywed women move into their parents-in-law's household. The excess workload in this phase of life affects time available for leisure, with young women having half as much available as compared to young men. Time that women dedicate to leisure and socializing, however, increases steadily with age, and women aged 60 and older are the group best placed in terms of available time for these activities, even compared to older men.

Decision-making on the allocation of household income also points at a changing role of women in different phases of their life. Adult married men are the main decision makers on household income in roughly one out of three cases, while women take these decisions on their own only when there are no adult men in the family, e.g., a family made of a widow and her children. Women have higher chances of taking part in decision-making in more egalitarian households where decisions are taken jointly, either by the main married couple or by different household members. Women also have higher chances of being one of the main decision makers as they get older. This is associated with existing cultural norms that assign elderly women an increasingly powerful role both in the household and the wider social sphere. In addition, it is more common for women in their 60s or older to be widowed than for men, due to a significant gender disparity in life expectancy in favor of women, so women often become head of the household in cooperation with their older son.

As time use data showed, women in their 60s or older still have a lot of household responsibilities, but they tend to shift toward household management tasks, care of grandchildren, and other types of emotional care: elderly women assign tasks to different household members and they also perceived as the "guarantors of peace and good family relations."

As regards politics, women's participation in community organizations is very low, but almost four out of five women voted in the last general elections. Qualitative interviews showed that older women (mostly in their 50s) who are well-off and relatively educated have higher chances of participating in community organizations and local government structures.

B.   Recommendations

The unequal distribution of unpaid work within households is one of the main causes of gender inequalities in labor market outcomes. An egalitarian distribution of unpaid care work among men and women is therefore key to gender equality. This needs to be complemented by equal access to paid and decent work to achieve women's economic empowerment and inclusive growth, as it is the interaction of gender disparities in time use with employment segregation that traps women in unpaid and low-paying work.

Breaking out of this trap requires interventions that lift time constraints, increase access to the job market, and correct the gender blindness of markets and institutions.

The recommendations outlined below focus on the first policy area, as measures needed to increase women's access to the job market and address the gender biases inherent in markets and institutions fall well beyond the scope of this study.[56]

To lift time constraints, action is required on three different areas: investment in social care and social assistance, changing social norms, and application of the legal framework for gender equality.

As widely recognized by gender advocates, one of the most effective strategies to reduce and redistribute unpaid and domestic work is public investment that addresses welfare needs, including social care, that provides universally accessible, high-quality care services, and social assistance, like cash transfers to women which have the potential to increase access to finance and allow women to manage finances.

Social care, and particularly childcare, provides a way to relax constraints on women's time. The evidence available for diverse countries worldwide highlights the need to design systems that can effectively address the needs of those groups of women who face barriers to labor market participation because they lack childcare. Hence, a detailed analysis of the care economy and of the gaps in the public provisioning of care services for various groups should be undertaken. This means looking in-depth into the availability of services for both pre-school and school-age children, along with the elderly, and persons with disabilities.

It is also important to note that most childcare delivery models have been tested in urban settings and less is known about what does and does not work in rural areas. It is therefore necessary to experiment in this area with a focus on delivery models that address the needs of rural women, who are most likely to use informal care arrangements. Attention should also be paid to the possibility of using the provision of childcare as an opportunity to create employment locally, while ensuring caregivers are adequately trained.

The main factor affecting gender roles in the household and the society, limiting women's agency and their discretionary time, are possibly social norms.

---

[56] The following documents were also consulted to formulate recommendations:
UN Women and UNDP. 2017. Investing in Social Care for Gender Equality and Inclusive Growth in Europe and Central Asia. Policy Brief. 2017/01.
World Bank. 2011. Gender Equality and Development. Washington, DC.
E. Rubiano–Matulevich and M. Viollaz. 2019. Gender Differences in Time Use Allocating Time between the Market and the Household. Policy Research Working Paper. No. 8981. Washington, DC: World Bank.

As seen above, in rural Tajikistan, traditional and patriarchal social norms strongly limit the decision-making power and autonomy of women, especially in the earlier phases of their adult lives. Women have to ask for permission to leave the house or to travel, in most households they have little say on how income is allocated, and they are responsible for an overwhelming majority of the unpaid work that is necessary to guarantee the reproduction and survival of their families.

Shifting the social norms that keep rural women in such a disempowered and vulnerable position is critical to combat time constraints and promote women's agency, but this process can be complex and slow. Policies, however, can help to change prevailing norms by providing incentives or information needed to challenge them.

To increase women's knowledge about alternatives to their daily reality, education, and media exposure are essential. Exposure to different models, including different female role models, and information on women's rights and existing opportunities can contribute to change social norms. This includes formal education, but especially other types of training and vocational courses for adults. Participating in women's committees and in informal groups can also contribute to change norms that restrict women's autonomy.

The survey showed that in the selected district, most women were not engaged in extra household activities. Their participation in water users' associations or other community groups was extremely limited, except for some older or more educated women. A broadening of women's networks should therefore be promoted, as well as women's participation in decision-making processes.

The policy and legal framework for gender equality clearly affects gender roles and agency. In Tajikistan, this framework includes a number of policies and pieces of legislation, particularly the 2011–2020 National Strategy to Promote the Role of Women in the Republic of Tajikistan, the 2005 Law on Sate Guarantees for Gender Equality, the 2013 Law on Domestic Violence, as well as a number of provisions contained in the Civil Code, the Labour Code, and Family Code, that protect women's rights and promote gender equality. In addition, in 2006, the Committee for Women's and Family Affairs was named as the state agency responsible for government policy on women's rights, family rights, and gender equality. This framework is considered solid, but it lacks clear implementation processes.[57] In practice, women face strong discrimination in accessing property and land, labor participation is low, and access to justice is problematic, especially in cases of psychological and economic violence against women. To improve women's agency and modify prevailing gender roles, existing legislation should be applied and enforced. It also has been pointed out that measures to facilitate access to justice for women, particularly in rural settings, should be developed and implemented.[58]

As mentioned above, even when women have time available, their decision (and possibly capacity) to allocate it to market work is subject to the existence of a well-functioning and open job market. Even though identifying measures to improve the rural job market in Tajikistan is beyond the scope of this study, it should be stressed that the creation of jobs that target rural women is imperative in a country like Tajikistan. Market forces can sometimes also weaken social norms by compensating for

[57] OECD. Social Institutions and Gender Index 2019, Tajikistan. https://www.genderindex.org/wp-content/uploads/files/datasheets/2019/TJ.pdf (accessed December 2019); ADB. 2016. *Tajikistan Country Gender Assessment*. Manila.

[58] UN Committee on the Elimination of Discrimination Against Women (CEDAW). 2013. Concluding Observations on the Combined Fourth and Fifth Periodic Reports of Tajikistan - CEDAW/C/TJK/CO/4-5, http://tbinternet.ohchr.org/_layouts/treatybodyexternal/Download.aspx?symbolno=CEDAW/C/TJK/CO/4-5&Lang=En.

the sanctions imposed for departing from them. For example, if women's earnings in labor markets are large enough, they can provide strong incentives for women to join them.

It could therefore be impactful to offer extension and training services that are specifically tailored to the needs of female farmers and entrepreneurs. Women's access to extension services and training should be promoted and the information and resources they provide should be relevant for female farmers. Mobile phones can be used as a platform for the delivery of information and services to rural populations, but, as the survey showed, there are significant gender gaps in access to mobile phones and the internet in rural Tajikistan, making access to information and communication technologies for women a potential area to explore.

Classification of Activities Used in the Survey

The reference activity classification used in this survey is a simplified adapted version of the ICATUS developed by the United Nations.

Table A1: Classification of Activities Used in the Survey

Code	Activity
11	Employment in corporations, government and non-profit institutions
121A	Growing wheat, cotton, fruit or vegetables for the market
121B	Growing other crops for the market
122	Raising animals for the market
1A	Other employment: construction, making goods, salesmen, repair, etc.
211	Growing crops (for own final use)
212	Farming animals and production of animal products (for own final use)
241	Gathering firewood (for own final use)
242	Fetching water (for own final use)
2A	Other activities for own final use, including house repair and maintenance
31	Cooking and making meals
32	Cleaning house and tidying up
34	Washing clothes and other textiles, shoes, mending and sewing
3A	Other domestic activities
41	Taking care of children
4A	Taking care of elderly, disabled or sick people, and other care activities
6A	Learning and studying
7A	Community activities and socializing
7B	Religious practice
8A	Culture and leisure: including watching TV, radio and other mass media, reading
91	Sleeping
92	Eating and drinking
9A	Washing oneself and other personal care, including medical care
T	Traveling

APPENDIX 2
A Focus on Women and Farming

Among other uses, this study will inform ADB's programming in Tajikistan, particularly an upcoming irrigation program. In this respect, a few indicators have been calculated based on the results of the time use survey.

Particularly as regards the production of cotton, wheat, and high-value crops, the disaggregated contribution of men and women in terms of time spent working on these crops is summarized in the following indicator:

- Time spent daily in rural areas on the production of wheat, cotton and high-value crops for the market disaggregated by sex—2019

The value of this indicator for women is equal to 1.2 hours (or 1 hour and 14 minutes); for men, it is approximately equal to 3.9 hours (or 3 hours and 52 minutes).

Figure A2.1: Time Spent Daily on the Production of Wheat, Cotton, and High-Value Crops for the Market Disaggregated by Sex
(hours)

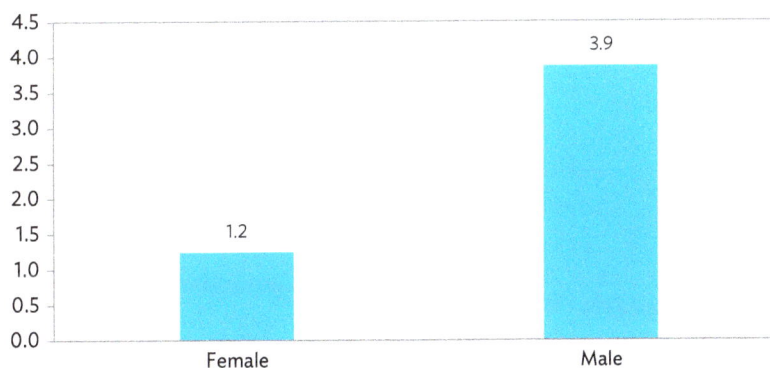

Source: Author's computation based on 2019 time use survey results.

As regards irrigation, the agricultural land that surveyed households have access to is in most cases (94%) only irrigated in part, which means that families might have a plot that is irrigated, including their home garden, and then other land that is not irrigated. Only 6% of households have irrigation on all their land. The method of irrigation is mostly traditional, but, in a handful of households, drip irrigation was also present, thanks to an international aid program.

Qualitative interviews showed that some people decide to return part of their non-irrigated land to the state when they are unable to make it profitable and it becomes a source of debt.

The participation of women and men in water users' associations can be characterized by the following indicators:

- Share of rural women participating in water users' associations—2019.
- Share of rural men participating in water users' association—2019.

The value of the indicator for women is equal to 0.9%, which is extremely low, while for men it is equal to 34%, i.e., about one in every three men.

Figure A2.2: Share of Rural Women and Men Participating in Water Users' Associations
(%)

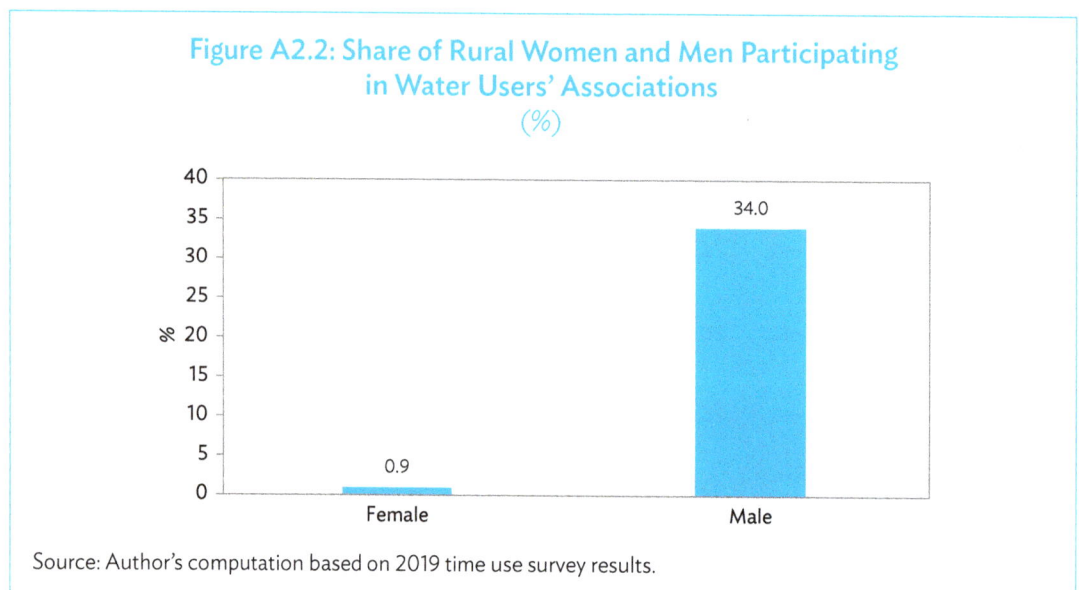

Source: Author's computation based on 2019 time use survey results.

It is worth noting that qualitative interviews confirmed this low level of participation. In Khuroson district, an older respected widowed woman, who headed a large household together with her older son, explained that even though she formally was a member of the water users' association, as the agricultural land was in her name, it was her son who usually participated. Another older woman residing in the same district explained she had acted as the head of the *mahalla* for many years, and, hence, also participated in water users' association.

The situation of this woman can in no way be considered typical in this area, but it is worth noting that she was in a position of power in her own household, even though her husband was still alive and living with her. This may well derive from the fact that the land was in this woman's name and that her husband used to be a driver, so she always was the one managing the farm.

APPENDIX 3
Participation Rates for Selected Activities

As explained in section III-D, indicators published by time use surveys are of three types. In this study, as in many time use surveys, it was decided to focus on the average daily time spent in a given activity by the total population, engaged or not in the activity.

However, in this appendix, participation rates for different types of labor are also provided, as a possibly useful reference for future gender-sensitive analysis and programming.

Participation rates express the number of people engaged in an activity divided by the total population—engaged or not—of the sample, regardless of the number of hours that they worked. Values for paid work, unpaid work for final use, and unpaid care and domestic work are provided in the table below.

Table A3: Participation Rates for Different Types of Work by Sex (%)

Type of Work	Female	Male
Paid work	43.6	85.8
Unpaid work for final use	83.6	81.1
Unpaid domestic and care work	99.1	53.6

Source: Author's computation based on 2019 time use survey results.

References

Asian Development Bank (ADB). 2016. *Tajikistan Country Gender Assessment*. Manila.

Agency on Statistics under President of the Republic of Tajikistan, Ministry of Health and Social Protection of Population of the Republic of Tajikistan, and ICF. 2018. *Tajikistan Demographic and Health Survey 2017*. Dushanbe and Rockville, Maryland.

Charmes, J. 2015. *Time Use Across the World: Findings of a World Compilation of Time Use Surveys*. Background Paper. New York: United Nations Development Programme (UNDP) Human Development Report Office.

Esquivel, V., D. Budlender, N. Folbre, and I. Hirway. 2008. Explorations: Time Use Surveys in the South. *Feminist Economics*. 14 (3). pp. 107–52.

Food and Agriculture Organization (FAO). 2016. *Gender Profile of Agricultural and Rural Livelihoods in Tajikistan*. Dushanbe: FAO.

Government of Tajikistan. 2015. *National Development Strategy*. Dushanbe.

Hirway, I. 2005. Integrating Unpaid Work into Development Policy. Paper presented at the Conference Unpaid Work and the Economy. New York: United Nations and Levy Economics Institute of Bard College.

Hirway, I. 2010. *Time-Use Surveys in Developing Countries: An Assessment*. https://www.researchgate.net/publication/304636246_Time-Use_Surveys_in_Developing_Countries_An_Assessment (accessed December 2019).

International Labour Organization (ILO). 2018. Survey Methods to Improve Measurement of Paid and Unpaid Work: Country Practices in Time-Use Measurement. Presented at the 20th International Conference of Labour Statisticians. Geneva: ILO.

ILO and UNDP. 2018. *Time-use Surveys and Statistics in Asia and the Pacific*. Geneva: ILO.

Kes, A. and H. Swaminathan. 2006. Gender and Time Poverty in Sub-Saharan Africa. In M. Blackden and Q. Wodon, eds. *Gender, Time Use and Poverty in Sub-Saharan Africa*. Washington, DC: The World Bank. pp. 13–38.

Maltseva, I. 2007. *Gender Equality in the Sphere of Employment*. Dushanbe: United Nations Development Fund for Women.

Öneş, U., E. Memis, and B. Kızılırmak. 2013. Poverty and Intra-Household Distribution of Work Time in Turkey: Analysis and Some Policy Implications. *Women's Studies International Forum*. 41. pp. 55–64.

Organisation for Economic Co-operation and Development (OECD). Social Institutions and Gender Index 2019, Tajikistan. https://www.genderindex.org/wp-content/uploads/files/datasheets/2019/TJ.pdf (accessed December 2019).

Oxfam GB. 2018. *Using Rapid Care Analysis to Account for Time Poverty in the Zarafshan Valley, Tajikistan*. Dushanbe.

Razavi, S. 2007. The Political and Social Economy of Care in a Development Context. *Gender and Development Programme Paper*. No. 3. Geneva: United Nations Research Institute for Social Development (UNRISD).

Ringhofer, L. 2015. Time, Labour, and the Household: Measuring "Time Poverty" through a Gender Lens. *Development in Practice*. 25 (3). pp. 321–332.

Rubiano-Matulevich, E., and M. Viollaz. 2019. Gender Differences in Time Use Allocating Time between the Market and the Household. *Policy Research Working Paper*. No. 8981. Washington, DC: The World Bank.

Singh, S., L. Ringhofer, W. Haas, F. Krausmann, and M. Fischer-Kowalski. 2010. Local Studies Manual: A Researcher's Guide for Investigating the Social Metabolism of Rural Systems. *Institute of Social Ecology Working Paper*. No. 120. Vienna: Institute of Social Ecology.

UN Committee on the Elimination of Discrimination Against Women (CEDAW). 2013. Concluding Observations on the Combined Fourth and Fifth Periodic Reports of Tajikistan - CEDAW/C/TJK/CO/4-5, http://tbinternet.ohchr.org/_layouts/treatybodyexternal/Download.aspx?symbolno=CEDAW/C/TJK/CO/4-5&Lang=En.

UNDP. 2019. *Human Development Report 2019*. New York.

United Nations Statistics Division (UNSD). 2005. *Guide to Producing Statistics on Time Use: Measuring Paid and Unpaid Work*. New York.

United Nations Statistics Division (UNSD). 2018. Modernizing Time Use Surveys. Presented at the International Forum on Gender Statistics. Tokyo.

UN Women and UNDP, 2017. Investing in Social Care for Gender Equality and Inclusive Growth in Europe and Central Asia. *Policy Brief*. 2017/01. New York: UN Women.

World Bank. 2011. *Gender Equality and Development*. Washington, DC.

World Bank. 2017. Tajikistan Jobs Diagnostic. *Jobs Series*. 1. Washington, DC. The World Bank. https://openknowledge.worldbank.org/handle/10986/26029 (accessed March 2020).

Zaman, H. 1995. Patterns of Activity and Use of Time in Rural Bangladesh: Class, Gender, and Seasonal Variations. *The Journal of Developing Areas*. 29 (3). pp. 371–388.